GOD'S SECRET PLACE

Also by Nate Stevens

Matched 4 Life (book and workbook)

Deck Time with Jesus

Transformed: Until Christ is Formed in You

Conformed: Into the Likeness of Christ

Informed: Living by God's Absolute Truth

GOD'S
SECRET
PLACE

Finding and Maintaining
Intimacy with God

NATE STEVENS

Acknowledgment

As a Christian author, it still amazes me how God continues to inspire and bless our human efforts to capture a message or vision from Him. How truly humbling to know, in spite of ourselves, He still anoints His Word, allowing it to fulfill His ultimate purposes. I do not take lightly the privilege and awesome responsibility of "rightly dividing" His truth. May God use this book to draw each reader into a closer, deeper, more intimate fellowship with Him.

Thank you, God, for awaiting us all in Your secret place.

Thank you, Andrea Merrell, for your editing expertise and encouragement. It is always great to learn new things. I appreciate your literary investment in me and this effort.

Thank you, Christine, for yet another superb cover concept. What an incredible gift to conceptualize the notions and "noodlings" in my head and make them a presentable reality.

Thank you, Russel Davis and Gray Dog Press, for your willingness and assistance in illustrative layout, formatting, and every other effort. May God bless you and your ministry.

Thank you, Karen Stevens, for inspiring the need and vision of this book's theme. The journey may be a lifetime, yet each day brings unique blessings and fulfillment. Thank you for walking the journey with me.

Oh, God, as I gaze across the crowded space of my mind, packed with assailing thoughts and distracting influences, help me see You, the Lover of my soul, Keeper of my spirit, and Renewer of my mind. Compel me to relentlessly fall in love with You. Discipline me to be undeterred, undistracted by all assaults in the battlefield of my mind. Restrict me from encouraging those storms to which You are speaking peace. Teach me how to be still in Your presence. Bring me to a place where You are my all in all. Amen.

Contents

Introduction ix

A Closer Walk with God 1

Ongoing Nearness to God 5

God's Secret Place 11

Time, Knowledge, Trust, and Vulnerability 19

Passionate Desire, Diligent Search 25

Overcoming Obstacles 29

The Battle for the Mind 39

Past Spiritual Failure Does Not Dictate Future Spiritual Success 45

Steps to Establishing Intimacy with God 51

Discovering Four Levels of Intimacy with God 59

What Determines the Difference Between Intimacy Levels? 65

Characteristics of Deepening Intimacy with God 71

Applying God's Promises 81

Realigning Personal Mindsets to God's Truth 89

Moving from Begging to Praising 99

Making the Commitment 107

Endnotes 111

About the Author 113

Introduction

How do I get to know God?

Once I get to know Him personally, how do I develop a deeper, more intimate relationship with Him?

Does God truly want intimacy with me or does He only get close to certain people in specific circumstances?

As the Almighty, Sovereign God, why would He want to have anything to do with insignificant me?

Is intimacy with God even attainable? I've tried several times, yet nothing seems to work—nothing changes.

Let's just say I do find out how to know God more deeply, what's in it for me?

I recently encountered these profound, penetrating questions when talking with someone about her personal walk with God. I had to admit, they are all excellent questions that deserve further time and consideration.

The first question seems relatively straightforward. *How do I get to know God?* We get to know God through salvation by faith in Jesus Christ. Jesus said, "No one comes to the Father except through Me" (John 14:6). He is the only way, the only truth. Only through Him do we have access to eternal, abundant life. We are saved by God's grace, through faith in Jesus—not through our own strength, efforts, or good deeds (Ephesians 2:8-9). This salvation happens only through spiritual rebirth "from above" (John 3:3, 7) and the indwelling of God's Holy Spirit (1 Corinthians 3:16). God's plan of salvation is clearly spelled out in His Word, the Bible. We will look at that more in depth a bit later.

The next set of questions requires serious consideration, reflection, and research. The triune God, creator of everything, eternal, uncreated, self-existing, omniscient, omnipotent, omnipresent, sovereign, King of kings, and Lord of lords … Wow! The mere concept of having a personal relationship with Him is overwhelming in and of itself. Then to think of establishing and nurturing a deepening interaction with Him—Mind. Blown. Away.

As difficult as it is to believe, the process of finding and maintaining an intimate, ongoing, deepening fellowship with God is available to everyone. But many powerfully influential factors affect it: human free will, personal desire, life circumstances, timing and priority, personal and spiritual discipline, past experiences, pain-points, and willingness to surrender to Him, to name just a few. It reminds me of the adage: Everybody wants to go to heaven, but no one wants to die. To most people, enjoying personal, sweet, intimate, and lifelong interaction with God Almighty *sounds* wonderful. Unfortunately, it seems few are willing to invest the time, energy, and effort for the rewarding journey.

And yet for those who long for such, I can attest from personal experience, it is well worth it. It is an experience—yes, lifestyle—that exceeds all others. To live with a constant awareness, ongoing dialogue, and continual interaction with God has become such a profound part of my life that I cannot recall life without it—nor would I want to live without it. I highly recommend it—and God desires it.

I am far from perfect. I do not claim to enjoy a daily flow of positive vibes in God's presence nor have I always lived with such sweet expectancy. There are days I displease my loving, heavenly Father and resist His ongoing efforts to transform me. But through His love, grace, mercy, forgiveness, and a myriad of other divine characteristics, He has brought me to where I can sit in His presence and exclaim, "I am my beloved's, and my beloved is mine" (Song of Solomon 6:3). I have learned to snuggle so close to Him that I can hear His heartbeat—then rest in His intimate fellowship.

So, if you are interested and willing, let's start the journey and walk through the process of finding and maintaining intimacy with God in His Secret Place.

Chapter 1

A Closer Walk with God

The struggle of finding and enjoying increasing intimacy with God is real. Every child of God, if being completely honest, faces two deep desires: a longing for deeper intimacy with God or the freedom from whatever keeps them from it. But no one is immune. The struggle is real.

When my children were infants, I would rock them to sleep. No matter how tired they were, they fought me—arching their backs, stiffening their legs, struggling against the very thing they needed most. I knew they were tired and needed to sleep. Many times, I would look down at them in my arms and wonder, *when are you going to just give it up?* They needed rest but resisted the process. But even though they fussed and struggled, as they rubbed their sleepy eyes, I held them close. The more they struggled, the more I lovingly held them to my chest. Within minutes, they stopped struggling, stopped resisting, and rested—fully surrendered—in the arms of their loving father.

I find this eerily similar to my struggle for intimacy with God. I indirectly resist His sweet communion with my non-stop prayer requests, complaints, worries, promise-claiming, and other vain babblings. It took me years to realize that what I desire most comes through what I fear the most—complete surrender. All the while, God faithfully and lovingly holds me closer to Himself. I suspect He also thinks, "Nate, when are you just going to surrender to Me?" Slowly but surely, I tire myself out, let go, and rest in His presence. Only when I stop talking can I hear His precious whisper. When I stop pushing my agenda, I sense His sweet presence. Realizing how woefully insignificant I am compared to God, I stop negotiating with Him and stand in awe of His invitation to walk

1

closer to Him, to enjoy a more acute awareness of His presence. I've found out the hard way there is no negotiation in surrender.

I also discovered my intimacy with God isn't something that, once attained, remains intact in perpetuity. If this were true, I wouldn't need scriptural encouragement to continue running my race (Hebrews 12:1), growing in the grace and knowledge of our Lord and Savior Jesus Christ (2 Peter 3:18), walking in the Spirit (Galatians 5:16), drawing closer to Him (James 4:8), diligently seeking Him (Hebrews 11:6), or constantly pressing forward in my Christian walk (Philippians 3:12-14). Like a fish in a river, I must either swim against the current or lazily float along with it. There is no "swimming in place" when it comes to intimacy with God.

The reality is an inner battle is raging between my carnal flesh and the indwelling Holy Spirit. They continually oppose each other "so that you do not do the things that you wish" (Galatians 5:17). Additionally, the world, its evil influences, and clamoring distractions swirl around me and also hinder my intimacy with God. Both inner and outer forces create a perfect vortex that challenges my closeness to Him. The noise from both realms threatens to drown out God's still, small voice. This reality motivates me to regularly reject my carnal desires—the old man—and consistently pursue the new man who is renewed each day (2 Corinthians 4:16). In a nutshell, this is the daily pursuit of intimacy with God.

By relating intimacy with God to a personal, authentic, intense, romantic relationship instead of a mystical, out-of-body experience, we might become more passionately involved in the pursuit. There would be no mind games, just having fun, or playing hard to get. Oh, no. When we are all in, our will, desires, passion, minds, and priorities become consumed with being in His presence. Not just during specific times, but an overriding, overwhelming, ongoing desire and awareness throughout each day.

Just as romantically involved people constantly interact with each other, God is the first person I want to talk with about any situation or event. He is the permanence that guides my thoughts. He is the focal point of my conversations. Each day, I direct my waking thoughts and bedtime prayers toward Him. Such intimate interaction makes my heart smile, sends peace to my soul, and gives direction to my life. Walking in the Spirit is no longer feared or forced; it becomes my natural pace.

Since mutual love is the essence of intimacy, and I know God loves me, any cooling of the relational warmth is of my own making. He cannot change who He is or His loving characteristic (Malachi 3:6). Any distance or cold breezes in my interaction with Him should prompt my quick return to the warmth of His embrace.

Face it, we all prioritize what is important. Very seldom, if ever, do we abandon our deepest desires, whether they involve careers, hobbies, business ventures, investments, or personal relationships. What is urgently important gets our undistracted attention. Like any relationship, we must prioritize, protect, and promote our relationship and ongoing interaction with God to achieve and maintain a deeper level of sweet fellowship with Him.

Chapter 2

Ongoing Nearness to God

For a better understanding of intimacy with God, we need to clearly define what it is and what it is not. Then we need to determine what it involves and why we should want to draw closer to Him.

To start with, consider the word *nearness*. It means proximity, closeness, or the lack of distance between two or more objects. It applies to the physical realm as well as the intellectual, emotional, and spiritual realms. People in agreement or of the same mindset have a sense of *mental* nearness. Those who are in romantic relationships experience a connection or *emotional* nearness. Individuals of the same faith or beliefs share a sense of *spiritual* nearness. The shared commonalities and experiences in each realm draw people closer together. By exploring those common bonds deeper, they strengthen a sense of togetherness and resulting intimacy of association.

Nearness also spans time and space—yes, entering the very throne room of God. We consider future, expected events as drawing near. For example, the Bible tells us, "The day of the LORD *is* near" (Ezekiel 30:3). Also, the future judgment of God in the valley of Jehoshaphat is getting closer. "The day of the LORD *is* near in the valley of decision" (Joel 3:14). Traveling through the vast expanse of space brings us closer to planets, stars, or other cosmic bodies. And yet a day draws near when God will "gather us all together from wherever we are—in heaven or on earth—to be with him in Christ forever" (Ephesians 1:10 TLB). That will be unmatched, eternal nearness. Through every realm and aspect of life, we find the constant theme of the nearness of the presence of God. As omnipresent, He is everywhere. We simply need to get closer to His heart.

5

God's Word speaks specifically regarding His proximity. "You are near, O LORD (Psalm 119:151). Jesus promised to be right beside us always (Matthew 28:20). God wants us to draw near to Him for our overall good (Psalm 73:28). He invites us to come near to Him with a sense of urgency and immediacy—"Seek the LORD while He may be found, call upon Him while He is near" (Isaiah 55:6). He promises to be near those who come close to Him (James 4:8) and is especially close to the brokenhearted and crushed in spirit (Psalm 34:18). He also knows the difference between those who draw near with mere lip service and those who earnestly desire intimacy from the heart (Isaiah 29:13). He promises to draw near to those who call upon Him truthfully, genuinely (Psalm 145:18). Even human relationships with those who merely talk a good game are superficial and unreliable.

The awesome news is the invitation for sincere nearness and intimacy with God goes out to everyone. "Let us draw near with a true heart in full assurance of faith…" (Hebrews 10:22). To accept that call is to enjoy a closer connection, conversation, and communion with God. To ignore or postpone it is to miss out on the most precious, most divine sense of love, wisdom, acceptance, fulfillment, and satisfaction.

What it is and What it is Not

Every person is different. Based on individual differences in spiritual maturity, desire, and priority (and sometimes circumstances), the journey to intimacy with God will look and feel different for each person. Although we can rejoice with each other for our individual glorious experiences, it is unwise to compare or measure ourselves based on our different journeys (2 Corinthians 10:12). Our goal should be to "run with endurance the race that is set before us, looking unto Jesus" (Hebrews 12:1-2) and him alone.

As we begin the journey toward deeper intimacy with Him, the first step is to recognize who He is and what His Word says. He is loving, but He is also holy. As the only true and living, eternal, self-existing, sovereign, almighty God, He deserves our awe and reverence. Approaching God is always a big deal. There is nothing frivolous about entering God's presence. Simply reading about the grandeur and majesty of His throne room (Revelation 4) should promote our wonder and worship.

That said, getting closer to Him doesn't require cleaning up our act, meeting a laundry list of good deeds, or developing impressive qualifications. As Mary, the sister of Martha and Lazarus, we can simply sit at His feet, lingering in His presence, listening to His words, absorbing His essence (Luke 10:39). All we need is a willing heart, prioritized time, a surrendered spirit, and an open, uncluttered mind. The desire to hear *from* Him, learn *about* Him, and become more and more *like* Him involves an intense longing to spend time in His presence, with His Word, listening to His Spirit's whisper. We find the same burning desire in romantic relationships. We develop a sense of nearness by spending time together, listening, sharing, learning, memorizing, simply enjoying each other's presence, closeness, and deepening intimacy. How amazing is that? Along with giving us His Word and Himself, God gives us relatable human experiences to help us understand and develop our experiences with Him.

This approach differs widely from what some people may consider as getting closer and spending quality time in God's presence. True nearness isn't simply sitting in church a couple hours each week. Nor is it reading through the Bible at a mandated pace to keep track with a reading program. Surprisingly, burning ourselves out doing a variety of obligated good deeds or service in ministry can still leave considerable distance from God. All these are a part of developing deeper intimacy with Him. But many times, our *doing* prevents our *being*. If a wife spent all her time running errands or hanging out with the girls, what time is there for simply *being* with her husband? If a husband spent all his time playing golf with his buddies or attending sporting events, what unstructured, spontaneous, prioritized time does he have for *being* with his wife?

In the story of Mary and Martha, Martha was *doing*, Mary was *being*. Jesus said only one thing was needed and Mary had chosen "that good part, which will not be taken away from her" (Luke 10:42). *Doing* may be necessary in a relationship; *being* is essential for deepening intimacy. Two people in a relationship can *do* all the usual relational activities but they won't have intimacy without *being*.

This same doing-being concept applies to our relationship and fellowship with God. If all we offer Him is a few rushed minutes each morning or evening, the intimacy of our fellowship suffers and will certainly not grow deeper. If all we offer Him is church attendance once a week, our level of intimacy with Him grows no deeper than the intimacy of spouses who only spend one hour together each week.

As another interesting correlation regarding the concept of nearness, the Hebrew word for marital sexual intimacy (*yada*) means "to know and be known deeply." Far deeper than merely knowing many facts or even sharing sexual pleasure, true intimacy is intended to plunge deeper—to each person's very essence. At the center of each person is a core waiting to be discovered and explored. This core discovery is the depth of intimacy, nearness, and closeness God wants with each of us. He is omniscient and already knows us completely. But He wants us to discover and explore Him deeply—through reading His Word and listening to His Holy Spirit. He wants us to uncover His heart, thoughts, ways, purposes, and immense love for us. As a groom longs for exclusive closeness with his bride, so God longs for exclusive closeness with us.

Intimacy Involves Personal Sacrifice

For those sincerely wanting an abiding, deepening, sweet level of intimacy with God, it will require sacrifice. Sacrifice of time, priority, responsibilities, vulnerability, and honesty. As an example, King David wanted a certain piece of property on which to build an altar to God. The owner willingly offered it to David for free. But David refused such a gracious offer because he wouldn't offer to God that which cost him nothing (2 Samuel 24:24).

There is a personal cost to drawing near to God. Such cost usually involves a change from life as we know it. It may mean getting up an hour earlier each day or giving up golf weekends. It could mean replacing Thursday girls' night with time spent in Bible reading and prayer. Maybe even exchanging *me time* for service to others as unto God Himself. Quite frankly, it could even involve separation from emotionally draining, time-consuming friendships to regain and repurpose time better spent in God's presence. As an example, people in successful romantic relationships yield personal preferences and likes in deference to their loved ones. God deserves no less.

As our supreme example, Jesus lovingly sacrificed everything to have a relationship with us. He emptied Himself of His heavenly glory, humbled Himself to walk among us as a human, and became obedient to the excruciating experience of the cross (Philippians 2:8). Why? Because He loves us. Because He wants an intimate relationship and ongoing nearness with us. Because only through Him can we enjoy eternal life with Him in the hereafter (John 14:1-3) and the abundant, fulfilling life He offers here and now (John 10:10). He sacrificed everything and offers us everything. How can we not sacrifice prioritized time to draw closer to Him each day?

Why Should We Want to Draw Near to Him?

Of course, there is no mandate to get closer to God. He gives us the free will to choose for or against Him—to grow closer to Him each day or not. We can continue doing things as we are, but we miss out on the incredible experience of living daily with an intense awareness of the awesome presence of Almighty God. Just as personal, earthly relationships stagnate without quality time and priority, our relationship and fellowship with God stagnates when we fail to invest significant time in it and make it a priority.

Once a person is saved, with the Holy Spirit living inside, a personal relationship with God does exist. But deeper connectedness and sweet fellowship only happen through a deliberate journey of deepening intimacy, continued discovery, and ongoing surrender. Even the most romantic, passionate couples, should they fail to value, prioritize, safeguard, and deepen their relationships, will experience distance, disconnectedness, temptation, and possibly even irreconcilable differences.

Jesus warned the disciples in the Garden of Gethsemane, "Watch and pray, lest you enter into temptation. The spirit indeed is willing, but the flesh is weak" (Matthew 26:41). The parallel meaning for our context is clear. "Pay attention! Remain alert! Though your head and heart may want something, the everyday routine and responsibilities often crowd out what is important. Choose today to prioritize your relationship with Jesus."

God calls us to draw near, to prioritize, to set aside specific time to nurture the relationship and deepen the intimacy with the One who loves us, offers us everything we need, promises to meet with us, and wants to prepare us for an eternity with Him. He has answers to every question, situation, and circumstance we face. In every aspect of our lives, He wants to share His wisdom, love, and direction. He longs to embrace us in the warmth and comfort of His presence. Most importantly, He desires to transform our lives as only He can—which only occurs through growing intimacy with Him. These are just some of the reasons why we should want to draw near to Him.

Welcome to the journey.

Chapter 3

God's Secret Place

A time of personal prayer is much different than deepening intimacy with God.

Regarding private prayer time, Jesus said, "When you pray, go into your room, and when you have shut your door, pray to your Father who is in the secret place" (Matthew 6:6). Prayer time can be a *part* of the intimate journey with God. It is there, in our private, secret places where we get alone with God and pour out our hearts to Him. But intimacy is more than spending time in prayer. It is an ongoing lifestyle, a deepening awareness and closeness with God.

Think again of a romantic couple. There are specific times for private, heart-to-heart conversations. But connectedness is something they constantly nurture. Their hearts and minds are connected. They are joined in purpose. They enjoy being together without having to say anything. Simply being in each other's presence is a fulfilling experience. It is comparable to an us-against-the-world mentality. They have the inside story. They know the punchline and are laughing together while everyone else is still waiting for the joke. What they share is an ongoing secret. To them, nearness is a state of being. They grow closer together simply by spending quality time together.

These parallels help distinguish between prayer time and intimacy. Prayer time is specific time set aside to worship God, praise Him, and present our requests before Him. Intimacy is a secret place—a hiding place—of constantly abiding in Him. It is an ongoing sense of His presence, an awareness of His nearness. In that place, we "pray without ceasing" (1 Thessalonians 5:17), but the purpose isn't to *do* but to *be* in His presence. It is the proving ground for eternity where His followers will be forever in His direct and immediate presence.

To some, this may be a foreign concept as they never cultivated such nearness here on earth with other people much less with God. For those who earnestly desire the intimacy of God's presence, God meets them in His secret place.

> *He who dwells in the secret place of the Most High shall abide under the shadow of the Almighty. I will say of the Lord, "He is my refuge and my fortress; my God, in Him I will trust." (Psalm 91:1-2)*

Several words in these verses deserve closer attention to fully grasp the deeper significance of God's secret place. A *secret* place is a private location that is covered, concealed, disguised, hidden, and protected. The word *shadow* implies a shaded or defended place. Both words give a sense of privacy, protection, and peace. From this we find that an intimate relationship with God offers secrecy, serenity, safety, and solitude.

Shade also implies proximity. To be in the shade of a tree, we must get close to the tree or beneath its branches. The same applies to God's shelter. We must get closer to Him than ever before. In His secret place, "He shall cover you with His feathers, and under His wings you shall take refuge; His truth shall be your shield and buckler. You shall not be afraid of the terror by night, nor of the arrow that flies by day" (Psalm 91:4-5). Embracing Him and taking shelter in His shadow is our safe place. "The LORD *is* your keeper (protector): the LORD *is* your shade at your right hand" (Psalm 121:5, parenthesis added). His presence is a safe refuge to all who go there, surrender to Him, and rest.

The word *dwell* means to continue, endure, inhabit, or sit down. *Abide* means to remain, spend the night, or reside permanently. In essence, when we routinely inhabit or sit in God's secret place, we remain permanently under His shadow. By staying faithful to the passionate pursuit of His intimacy, we stay close to Him. As further confirmation, we have His promises on the matter. He is near to all who call upon Him in truth (Psalm 145:18). The closer we get to Him, the closer He gets to us (James 4:8).

Both words—dwell and abide—confirm God's immediate, surrounding, residing presence with us.

When I pursue His presence, I sense Him in all I do. I am aware of His active engagement and sovereign orchestration in my life. I see evidence of His handiwork everywhere. I live more circumspectly because I know He walks beside me. But when I move out of His shade, when I become lethargic in my journey and stray from Him, I feel the disconnectedness. He is still there, but our fellowship suffers. The resulting distance discomforts me as much as the nearness comforts me. Only when I return to His secret place do I sense the warmth rush back into our relationship and fellowship.

Moving on to the next word of importance, we find the word *refuge*. This implies a secure place of hope and trust. In the Old Testament, several cities were designated as cities of refuge where a person could find sanctuary from adversaries or await his day in court. The word *fortress* defines a place of capture, safety, and defense, as in a castle or stronghold. Solomon wrote, "The name of the LORD *is* a strong tower; the righteous run to it and are safe" (Proverbs 18:10). The word *safe* means secure or set on high. The word translated as *LORD* is actually Jehovah—God's name that combines the three tenses of the verb "to be." As Jehovah, God reveals Himself, and meets with us, as the One who was, is, and is to be.[1] When we run into God's presence, we find safe shelter within the almighty, eternal I AM. Augustus Toplady (1776) described this magnificently by writing, "Rock of Ages, cleft for me, let me hide myself in Thee."[2]

Both *refuge* and *fortress* describe God's intimate presence as a safe, secure sanctuary where we are safe to become vulnerable with Him. No foe is there to accuse us; no fear can assail us. In reality, we could describe it as the place where we allow God to capture us, regardless of our imperfections, doubts, and inadequacies. As counterintuitive as it may seem, we enter His safe and intimate stronghold by surrendering to Him. May we run across the drawbridge and into the fortress with arms raised in surrender. Only there, in that manner, are we truly secure. Jesus said, "You did not choose Me, but I chose you" (John 15:16). As His chosen love interest, we must stop playing hard to get and open our hearts to His loving pursuit and capture. Instead of resisting or forgetting our "resting place" (Isaiah 50:6), may we ever find our rest, refuge, and safety in Him.

The final word to examine is *trust*. It means to be bold, confident, secure, or carefree. Trust implies complete reliability in someone or something. When we drive across a bridge, we trust it as a dependable means to cross over whatever is below. By confiding in someone, we trust them to reliably safeguard whatever we have shared with them.

But there is one major challenge. It is difficult to trust the unknown or to trust when we are afraid. Trust implies intimate knowledge and deliberate vulnerability to go beyond superficial acquaintance and into true intimacy. To enter into this with God, we must trust Him implicitly. In trusting Him, we must believe He loves us and has our best interests at heart. To genuinely believe this leads us to cast aside our fear and surrender to Him. We realize it is okay to lower our defenses with Him. After all, He already knows us better than we know ourselves. Whatever trace of freewill we grasp as defiant or protective only confirms our lack of trust. It also prevents the intimacy we seek. Far better it is to fully trust, release "every weight, and the sin that so easily ensnares" (Hebrews 12:1), and faithfully find shelter in the secrecy, serenity, safety, and solitude of God's presence.

A Place of Peaceful Communion

With the onslaught of the Corona pandemic in late 2019, several governing bodies and *expert* authorities advised everyone to shelter in place beginning in early 2020. They cautioned people to stay at home as much as they could to avoid possible exposure to the virus. Hidden away in the safety and security—and isolation—of our homes, we would be protected from potential contamination. In much the same way, those seeking intimacy with God shelter in place in His presence to avoid exposure to the evil effects and contamination of this sinful world. By hiding and abiding in God's intimacy ("your life is hidden in Christ" Colossians 3:3), we find safety and rest in His shade ("you will find rest for your souls" Matthew 11:29).

The description God gives in Psalm 91:1-2 is that of a secret, hidden place. A place of peaceful rest in the shade. Both concepts are difficult to resist—especially for exhausted, parched souls. When considering them together, they paint a picture of a comforting, quiet, safe haven. An intimate refuge that offers an escape from the noise, chaos, and nastiness of life. A place where we can relax, let down our guards, and be completely open and honest without fear of unmet expectations, judgment, or disapproval. As a loving Father, God's counsel during the shared, isolated, quiet times is for our protection, benefit, and ongoing development.

Intimacy, by definition, implies a close, safeguarded, private, prioritized, and valued relationship. Such a relationship involves individuals who mutually share the safety of exclusive enjoyment, relaxation, protection, and privacy. Think of a romantic relationship. It is one that both people enjoy. Both can relax with each other, let down their guards, and be progressively vulnerable within the protection and privacy their relationship offers—and demands. God desires this and awaits you in His secret place.

Yesterday Affects Today, But Tomorrow Can Be Better

One major frustration within personal relationships is not having or being able to find peaceful, enjoyable, exclusive closeness. For example, insufficient time together may be the enemy. Or each person may be at different emotional levels where connection is resisted or impossible. One person may long for such closeness while the other is completely content with the convenience of a superficial relationship. Lack of intimacy results from a myriad of factors. And yet such closeness is a core relational ingredient. In its absence, human relationships either don't last or they simply bob along in the shallow waters of convenience.

Unfortunately, this same struggle for intimacy exists in the relationship and fellowship with God.

As flawed human beings, today is the result of all our yesterdays—good and bad alike. Likewise, our current mindsets are formed by past experiences. If they were good experiences, we develop a naturally good outlook while expecting life to continue providing good experiences. Unfortunately, bad past experiences can have a paralyzing effect. For example, if authority figures in a man's life have disappointed, abused, or abandoned him, he may overlay those negative perceptions onto bosses, ministry leaders, and even God. If a woman was a victim of abuse, her survival skills, self-preservation, and protective measures kick into overdrive and may negatively affect her interactions with potential dates and her future husband. These human tragedies and similar situations create trust issues. And yet trust is foundational to relational intimacy. No trust, no intimacy.

Thankfully, our tomorrows are determined by our decisions today. Today, we can decide to change any flawed mindsets or hindrances from the past. We can choose to walk "in newness of life" (Romans 6:4) with our minds renewed by God (Romans 12:2). Today can be the start of the amazing journey toward the secret, safe, secure, and serene place of intimacy with God.

Have you Spent the Night with Jesus?

I meditate on You in the night watches. (Psalm 63:6)
I remember Your name in the night, O Lord (Psalm 119:55)
Jesus … spent the night praying to God. (Luke 6:12, NIV)

Followers of Jesus Christ are wise to spend more time with Him in prayer. He alone can deliver. He alone holds tomorrow in His hand of sovereign orchestration. Only in Him do we find forgiveness for the past, strength for present troubles, and courage for future uncertainty. In Him alone do we find the transforming power to become more like Him.

Several years ago, God gave me the following message regarding my own journey of intimacy with Him.

> Have you spent the night with Jesus?
> Did you give yourself to prayer?
> All the cares of life abandoned,
> Did you haste or linger there?

In the silence of the evening,
Have you heard Him call your name
To that quiet place of solace?
Did you tarry—heart aflame?

Have you wrestled long past midnight,
Undeterred to see His face?
In the stillness of the darkness
Have you found His warm embrace?

Have you heard Him whisper softly,
His sweet truth your cares dispel?
Have you knelt beside His altar
'Til He bid your fears farewell?

Have you ventured in the battle
To the place where angels trod?
With your tears so freely streaming,
Have you grasped the throne of God?

Will the dawning of the morning
Find you weary, worn, and spent?
All your cares perfumed with mercy,
Your hands tinged with Heaven's scent?

As night shadows yield to daylight
Does your heart His image bear?
Do you more resemble Jesus
Having spent the night in prayer?

Nate Stevens
November 12, 2012

Chapter 4

Time, Knowledge, Trust, and Vulnerability

Successful relationships are based on quality time, intimate knowledge of each other, mutual trust, and vulnerability. That is, after all, the reason why we seek relationships. Who in their right mind wants a relationship where no time is spent together, no personal information is mutually shared, neither person trusts the other, and neither feel safe being vulnerable? We already have all those restrictions as individuals outside of relationships. What's the point to having a relationship if we cannot also have these critical qualities?

But as much as we seek and cherish them, the pathway to these foundational elements is sequential. They don't happen all at once. People normally don't become vulnerable with others before establishing a certain level of trust. And we generally don't trust until we get to know someone and determine his or her level of trustworthiness. Furthermore, we cannot truly know someone until we spend considerable time together. Time builds knowledge, knowledge enables trust (or distrust), and trust promotes vulnerability. The more we know, the more we trust (or distrust). The more we trust, the more willing we are to become vulnerable. The more vulnerable we become, the closer the connection. And the closer the connection, the more intimate the relationship.

Now, apply that sequential order to an intimate relationship with God. When we truly get to know God's loving, gracious, tender, faithful, and loyal character, we find that we can trust Him. Trust runs proportional to our knowledge and acceptance of who He is—His unchanging character, heart, purpose, promises, intent, essence, and so on. Once we get to know Him personally and not simply know *about* Him, we feel safe enough to open ourselves up and become vulnerable with Him. Becoming more vulnerable with Him—exposing our true inner selves—deepens the nearness.

To help visualize the essence of truly trusting, imagine yourself standing next to a chair. You can passionately *believe* the chair will support you. But you only demonstrate *trust* when you sit in it, relying on it to support your weight. Even then, your trust level is suspicious if you white-knuckle the armrests, ready to stand should the chair even squeak. That is a predisposed I-knew-it-would-fail mindset, not trust. On the other hand, you fully trust by relaxing in the chair, leaning back, lifting your feet, and relying on the chair to support you. Taking the analogy a step further, vulnerability is where you relax in the chair without an anxious thought or care of falling. You trust it and don't give it a second thought. Of course, your trust, reliance, and vulnerability may depend on previous experiences with other chairs. If, in your past, one or two chairs broke and sent you sprawling, you may find it a bit unnerving to completely trust this chair.

Consider this analogy from the perspective of developing intimacy with God. Even though God is completely trustworthy, sometimes intimacy with Him is still lacking and difficult to establish. Getting to know who He is often leads us to understand the struggle for deeper connectedness with Him lies within ourselves.

Picture yourself in a human relationship with someone absolutely wonderful, loving, responsible, reputable, committed, and with unques-tioned integrity. This person loves, honors, and admires you intensely, is faithfully devoted to you, and wants to spend the rest of his or her life with you. If you fiercely love this person, yet relational intimacy suffers, it would seem natural to look within. You would have to ask what restricts you. Doubt? Fear? Mistrust from past broken relationships? Protection against past hurts? Disappointment from past unmet expectations? Until you find that barrier, true intimacy will remain elusive.

If the relationship is important to you both, these issues require much more dialogue. You would need to talk through whatever hinders the progression to a deeper level of intimacy. Meaning, more time together is necessary. Both should invest time together, slowly and honestly revealing more and more of yourselves to discover what blocks deeper intimacy.

Granted, some relational issues are insurmountable while others are possible to overcome. Liking instead of loving someone or not having an emotional connection are common dealbreakers. But for those issues that *can* be overcome, time and discussion help reveal and resolve them. For example, a person who has been abused, victimized, disappointed, or abandoned undoubtedly will have more difficulty trusting, being vulnerable, and relinquishing control than someone who has never endured such trauma. Through discussion, openness, understanding, and healing, this issue can be resolved for the sake of the relationship.

In many ways, similar unresolved pain restricts our intimacy with God. But surrendering our will, mindsets, and pain to God and resting in His quiet place requires that very level of trust and release. Past painful, unhealed, or even unsurrendered experiences may be the obstacles keeping us from drawing closer to God. As a result, a traumatized person may take longer to establish and enjoy intimacy with God—barring supernatural intervention and divine healing. But with the breakthrough comes fierce loyalty and undying trust.

Until we are healed from past relationship pain points, how can we recognize, pursue, and interact in a new, healthy relationship? Until we have healthy mindsets, how can we enjoy full vulnerability and intimacy with others, much less God? In not fully trusting God, we doubt His promises, protection, purposes, and good intention. Then, in that place of doubt, we conjure up countless negative thoughts and false imaginations and project them onto Him. *After all, why would He care about one single person? I am not worthy of His attention, affection, or time. Sure, He may be intimate with others, but He isn't with me. I know He exists, but I don't feel Him or sense His presence in my life.*

The disciples demonstrated such mistrust by confronting Jesus in the middle of a storm on the Sea of Galilee (Mark 4:35-41). They forgot He had previously asked them to set sail for the *other side* of the lake. His purpose was on the *other side*. As Sovereign God, He already knew about the coming storm before they even set sail. Yet He still prompted them to shove off from shore and head for deeper waters.

Most of the disciples were either fishermen by trade or at least acquainted with sailing as a form of travel. They knew the perils of stormy seas. To see their Master fast asleep in the middle of the whipping winds, crashing waves, and apparent danger made them question Him. "Do You not care that we perish?" Their past experiences and instinct prompted their current doubt, fear, and mistrust.

But Jesus awoke, calmed the storm, and subsequently challenged their fear and doubt. To paraphrase it, He asked, "Gentlemen, you know Me, have heard My teachings and claims, and have seen the miracles I perform. Why do you still doubt Me?"

If we had been there that day, some of our reactions might have been, "Sure, all those miracles were for other people, not us." Or "Yes, we've heard Your teachings and claims, but what good do they do if You're asleep while we drown?" At that time, they knew *about* Him, but they still hadn't come to a place of trusting Him—vulnerably relying on Him—no matter the situations (cascading waves) or circumstances (water splashing into the boat). Their doubt sprang from a lack of knowing Him *intimately* or applying what they did know about Him to themselves *personally*.

Such fear and doubt run contrary to God's essence. They contradict His promises and multiple instructions of "Fear not" in His Word. "You drew near on the day I called on You, and said, 'Do not fear!'" (Lamentations 3:57). Sure, we may read and familiarize ourselves with His Word. But due to past painful experiences and lack of trust, we discount His promises and disconnect from His intimacy. We fail to personalize or apply what He says. Little do we realize, by maintaining such mindsets, we play right into Satan's hand. Fear and doubt are two of his best weapons. He is the master deceiver and father of lies (John 8:44). As such, he seeks to steal, kill, and destroy (John 10:10). He has an aggressive strategy to destroy us (1 Peter 5:7). He hisses his stench, hoping to keep us from the very thing that ushers us into the intimacy with God that we so desperately seek and need.

In our fear, doubt, lack of trust, and absence of vulnerability, we frantically grasp the oars of the floundering ship of our lives, reach for the tattered sails, or white-knuckle the helms, all in the hopes of controlling, avoiding, or sailing out of our self-made isolation. Yet Jesus peacefully beckons us to trust Him, grab a deck pillow, stretch out on deck beside Him, snuggle up so close we can hear His heartbeat, and rest. Rest in His presence. Rest in His protection. Rest in His provision. Rest in His peace. Rest and trust in His secret place.

Admittedly, resting and trusting are very difficult in the chaos of life and lack of intimacy with God. Then again, intimacy is built on trust, and trust is a personal choice that depends on spending sufficient time getting to know someone's heart. How can we trust someone if we don't know his or her heart? That said, the journey of finding intimacy with God begins by knowing the heart of God. How deep is our desire to know it?

Chapter 5

Passionate Desire, Diligent Search

One thing I have desired of the LORD, that will I seek: that I may dwell in the house of the LORD all the days of my life, to behold the beauty of the LORD, and to inquire in His temple. (Psalm 27:4)

The pursuit of intimacy isn't a part-time or casual endeavor—not in human relationships nor with God. To change the famous adage slightly, something worth doing is worth doing passionately. "Whatever your hand finds to do, do it with your might" (Ecclesiastes 9:10). The strategic pursuit of getting to the heart of God should leave us breathless.

As king of Israel, David had many desires and distractions related to his kingdom. Everyday life involved legal proceedings, meeting with leaders, regal appearances, leading his army, spending time with family. Yet above it all, he had one consuming desire.

"One thing I have desired of the LORD."

It was a personal, prioritized, passionate pursuit. David longed to spend time in God's presence. He desired to experience God's beauty. He wanted to "worship the Lord in the beauty of holiness" (Psalm 29:2). To gaze upon God's beauty and be embraced in God's presence. No wonder he was called a man after God's own heart (Acts 13:22).

If we could have only one genuine experience in this setting, I suspect all other desires and priorities would melt away. No other earthly experience can compete. The sacredness and nearness of God Almighty dims and distances all other distractions and ambitions. In His presence is *fullness* of joy and eternal pleasures (Psalm 16:11).

As with anything valuable, finding and maintaining intimacy with God involves a diligent, passionate effort. We find very little treasure

25

floating at the ocean's surface. On the contrary, a diligent search for treasure involves intensive study and intentional strategy before diving into the ocean depths. Such a search would include researching all historical data—contents, location, and previous attempts to find it. Oceanography maps would need to be studied to determine currents and seascape. Time and money would need to be invested for a serious endeavor to find the treasure. Diligence involves intentionality and a serious, narrow, prioritized focus.

Finding Reliable Truth

Although we may be passionate, we can also be misguided. For that reason, we must be specific regarding the information we accept as reliable. The search for intimacy with God cannot embrace all sources of tolerated or perceived truth—even our own preconceived ideas of truth. That would be tantamount to scuba diving the entire ocean while looking for one specific object. Even though today's society promotes acceptance and tolerance of everyone's version of truth, in doing so we miss *the* Truth by thousands of miles. We could never cover the broad scope of trying to understand everyone's version of truth nor would we find what we were looking for.

To demonstrate the fallacy of accepting multiple versions of truth, imagine if five people held varying standards for the measurement of a foot. You gather them to discuss and *tolerate* their specific viewpoints. One might say, "A foot is eleven inches," while another would argue it was thirteen inches. Finding five different definitions of the measurement, it would be impossible to get agreement. Nor could you accept all versions of such individualized truth. Next, consider if you hired them as home builders. What kind of a mess would you have with the final product? This exaggerated analogy shows how ridiculous it is to accept various versions of truth when an *absolute standard* is available. In measurement, a foot is twelve inches. In math, two plus two will always equal four. People may have varying opinions, but there is no variation of *absolute* truth.

We must exercise great care to accept only reliable, verifiable, consistent, and unchanging sources of information. Since God is truth, all other options and opinions are futile that seek to find Him apart from His truth. The search for intimacy with God must use His truth exclusively. It is His truth, His whole truth, and nothing but His truth.

Relentless Pursuit by Determined Hearts

In addition to using only God's Word, drawing close to Him and maintaining intimacy with Him require strategic, passionate, relentless efforts by determined hearts who stop at nothing until they find rest in His presence. Only those who "hunger and thirst" for righteousness will be filled (Matthew 5:6). The desire must be all-compelling.

Any relationship worth having involves passion. Passion for the person, passion for the journey of getting to know him or her better, passion for his or her presence. Likewise, intimacy with God involves passion for Him, passion for the journey of getting to know Him, and passion for being in His presence.

Thankfully, God rewards those who diligently seek Him (Hebrews 11:6). This diligence implies a passionate craving or intense investigation until something or someone is found. A great example of relentless persistence is Thomas Edison in his pursuit of inventing the filament lightbulb. He made one thousand attempts before he finally succeeded. Many people seek after God but don't find Him. Why? Because their search is lethargic, misguided, or halfhearted. They give up too soon. They want the outcome but hesitate on the journey. Jesus confirmed only a few people would push through the exclusivity and effort of the process. "Narrow is the gate and difficult is the way which leads to life, and there are few who find it" (Matthew 7:14). Though the journey may be challenging, it is available to all and rewarding to those who find it. And we have a standing invitation from Jesus: "Come to Me, all you who labor and are heavy laden, and I will give you rest" (Matthew 11:28).

A genuine search for intimacy with God exceeds mere enthusiasm or momentary emotionalism. Periodic emotional experiences simply cannot compare with an ongoing, energizing, deepening intimacy. Referring back to a romantic relationship, imagine valuing higher a few passionate embraces instead of a lifelong intimate relationship. The embraces may be powerful and sensational. But they are temporary moments in time. Establishing and maintaining the intimate relationship includes many such passionate embraces and a whole lot more.

Such a diligent, passionate quest to know God and be fully known by Him is a prioritized, desperate, and relentless pursuit that is quenched by nothing else. "As the deer pants for the water brooks, so pants my soul for You, O God" (Psalm 42:1). Intimacy with God is the ultimate goal. We must want it more than anything else and continue to be persistent on the journey. Similar to Jacob, may we pray, "I will not let You go unless You bless me!" (Genesis 32:26). This tenacious panting, craving, and longing for God is the gateway to His promised reward—His sweet presence. "And the Lord, whom you seek, will suddenly come to His temple, even the Messenger of the covenant, in whom you delight" (Malachi 3:1). As His followers, we are the temple of God (1 Corinthians 3:16). When we seek Him, He suddenly responds. "Ask, and it will be given to you; seek, and you will find; knock, and it will be opened to you" (Matthew 7:7).

When we realize, apart from God, everything in this world is empty, temporary, insignificant, and unsatisfactory, our journey becomes desperate. Like the prodigal son (Luke 15:11:21) in the "far off country" away from his father, only when we come to our senses do we realize all our rest, resources, and rewards are found with our loving, heavenly Father. May we passionately and diligently ask, seek, and knock in our pursuit of intimacy with Him.

Chapter 6

Overcoming Obstacles

Numerous obstacles can restrict intimacy in any relationship. Lack of passion, insufficient time together, distracting priorities, routine responsibilities, lack of common ground, absence of transparency, selfishness, and trust issues to name just a few. The list is as long and unique as the complexity of each person. The same obstacles also apply to intimacy with God. By recognizing them, we can address and resolve them. Let's look at a few obstacles that are most recognizable and highly impactful to our journey.

Insufficient Time in God's Word

Most lovers read and reread the cards, love letters, or notes they exchange. They cherish them, reference them often, linger over their words and meaning, and keep them close for immediate access. Sometimes they even carry them along in their daily routines. If sprayed with cologne or perfume, lovers frequently smell those love letters while fond memories dance across the theaters of their minds. Sharing such romantic letters, cards, or notes with others is also a matter of affection and devotion.

Imagine if we treated God's Word with such dedicated passion. This doesn't mean an obligated, regimented daily reading of one or two chapters. Nor does it imply spending two hours reading His Word so we can check it off a spiritual to-do list. Quantity never equates to quality. Spending quality time on a few verses can be much more meaningful and impactful than speed-reading through an entire book just to keep up with a Read-Through-the-Bible-in-a-Year calendar. When reading God's Word, a good rule of thumb is to consider what it says, what it means, and how it applies personally. Take your time with God's Word. Cherish it. Meditate on it. Research it. Memorize it. Pause while reading to allow the Holy Spirit to whisper some applicable truth. He is the Spirit of Truth who guides us into all truth (John 16:13). Give yourself time to think through what it means to you. Like a perfumed love letter, let its sweet fragrance permeate your heart, mind, and life.

But let's not become so infatuated with the written Word that we forget the Living Word. The love letter is but a reminder of the lover. Bible reading, studying, memorizing, analyzing—all of it—should point us to the Person behind the Word. Jesus Christ is the central theme. "So that they should seek the Lord, in the hope that they might grope for Him and find Him, though He is not far from each one of us; for in Him we live and move and have our being" (Acts 17:27-28). Love letters are the expressions of the person who gave them. God's written Word should direct our hearts and minds to the Living Word.

A dedicated passion for intimacy with God is when our hearts burn with an intense desire to spend *quality* time—sometimes even momentary encounters—with God's Word in His presence. Imagine how much more intimate our interaction with God becomes if we spent unrushed, thoughtful, quiet time reading and rereading His Word, then listening for the Holy Spirit's whisper. Just think how our closeness with Him would improve by valuing His Word as a personal love letter, taking it with us throughout our daily lives, and sharing it with others. After all, He sprayed it with His love, sealed it with His blood, and breathed it with His inspiration. What a dear treasure to be cherished.

Insufficient Time in God's Presence

Without quality time, intimate relationships suffer. Even long-distance relationships generally suffer from a lack of quality time together. When two people spend time together, they share heartfelt thoughts, behaviors, reactions, dreams, aspirations, motives, and commitment to each other. They feed off each other—reading facial expressions and body language, listening to both verbal and nonverbal communication. They begin trusting each other, revealing more and more of their true selves. To be clear, spending time together involves more than talking nonstop or constantly going from one activity to another. There is huge enjoyment simply *being* in each other's presence, snuggled together, just listening to each other breathe, hearing the pulse of each other's heart.

Now, consider how much more intimate the relationship with God becomes by spending quality time resting quietly in His presence—without filling the time with prayer requests, complaints, frustrations, or pouring out nonstop words. Usually when we're talking, we're not listening. How different would the time be if we were perfectly still in His presence (Psalm 46:10). Actually, the implication behind the words *be still* is to *shut up*. No relationship thrives with one-way, nonstop chatter. May we simply rest in His presence, away from the noise, distractions, and demands of life—yes, even from the mental circus going on in our heads.

Most romantic relationships don't survive without spending quality time together. Even if they do, they generally cannot thrive. Sometimes people take drastic measures to either strengthen the relationship, restore the relationship, or leave the relationship altogether. Desperate times require drastic measures. When something becomes urgent, it gets prioritized.

In the absence of spending quality quiet time with God and His Word, what drastic measures will He need to take to get our attention so He can spend quality time with us?

Insufficient Importance or Priority

No one likes to be taken advantage of or taken for granted. Imagine a lover who was never granted any time or prioritized consideration. Would he or she want to stay in a relationship of convenience? Would he or she accept a devalued status of no time or attention? Would constant interruptions or distractions from the relationship be acceptable? Probably not. Intimacy demands importance and priority—not based on forced obligation or duty, but on sheer love. Overwhelming love compels a lover to reject all others—people, places, things, hobbies, career—and focus on his or her beloved.

Imagine how such loving attention and urgency, coming from passionate and committed hearts, impacts intimacy with God. Such importance and priority are not merely shown during a ritual quiet time we carve out each day. On the contrary, it is a constant sense of nearness, an ongoing buzzing of mind, a lingering desire for Him. Acknowledging His active presence in our day-to-day activities builds an increased awareness of His constant involvement and sovereign orchestration in even the smallest details.

Unfortunately, we sometimes miss opportunities for intimate encounters with Him because they don't happen when and where we expect them. Waiting for His booming voice on demand, we miss His reassuring whisper in each sunset. Growing frustrated at His silence during our available quiet time, we miss His still, small voice while mowing the lawn, in the shower, or on a nature walk. He is always there, in every encounter, waiting for us to be still, to recognize Him, to rest in Him, and to give Him the importance and priority He deserves. If we look for Him, we will find Him. Everywhere.

Just as romantic lovers maintain a sense of each other throughout the day, true intimacy with God involves a constant sense of His presence. Starting each day with a tender, "Good morning, God." Sharing glorious sunrises and sunsets with Him. Thanking Him for every blessing, no matter how seemingly small or insignificant. Involving Him in every conversation. Telling Him our intimate thoughts, fears, victories, desires, disappointments, and heartaches. Expressing appreciation for *who* He is, not merely what He *does*. Rushing into His presence to praise Him. Quickly confessing failures and asking forgiveness. Being completely open and honest with Him. Honoring Him in all that is said and done. Such a nearness involves a constant conversation—praying without ceasing (1 Thessalonians 5:17). We acknowledge Him in all our ways (Proverbs 3:5-6). As with any passionate pursuit, we rejoice and revel in His presence (Psalm 16:11).

Resignation to Failure Based on Past Experience

There is no fear in love—perfect love removes fear (1 John 4:18). If we love Him and acknowledge that He loves us, then nothing can, or should be allowed to, separate us from loving intimacy with Him.

> *Who shall separate us from the love of Christ? Shall tribulation,*
> *or distress, or persecution, or famine, or nakedness, or peril, or*
> *sword? For I am persuaded that neither death nor life, nor angels*
> *nor principalities nor powers, nor things present nor things to come,*
> *nor height nor depth, nor any other created thing, shall be able to*
> *separate us from the love of God which is in Christ Jesus our Lord.*
> *(Romans 8:35, 38-39)*

Past heartbreak and rejection are very painful events. If they remain unhealed, they present real obstacles to loving or trusting again. Especially if they have happened more than once. Yet holding current people accountable for past failures is not fair—for anyone involved. When we fear intimacy in new relationships based on past rejection or betrayal, we remain bound in the prison of pain and isolation. Just because warmth and intimacy weren't a reality in the past doesn't mean we cannot experience it in the future.

This is where the similarity ends between intimacy with God and personal or romantic relationships. God has never failed, rejected, abandoned, or betrayed us—regardless of how we feel, no matter our misguided thoughts, blame, or bitterness toward Him for whatever reason. He doesn't change (Malachi 3:6), loves us beyond comprehension (John 3:16), and gives a peace in His presence that we cannot truly understand (Philippians 4:7). Instead of condemnation echoing in our ears, God promises overwhelming satisfaction for those whose "delight is in the law of the LORD, and in His law he meditates day and night" (Psalm 1:1-2). That is with whom we desire intimacy. A loving, faithful, reliable, unchanging God.

Imagine how much deeper our interaction with Him becomes when we stop projecting onto Him hurts and doubts from past failed human relationships. How much more endearing the nearness becomes by simply trusting who He is, accepting His unconditional, everlasting love, and personalizing His desire for intimacy with us.

Resistance to Full Transparency Resulting from Past Pain

Two people in a relationship only grow closer to the extent they drop their guards and open themselves up to each other. If one person safeguards or withholds even a small part of himself or herself, the other person senses it and grows frustrated with the exclusion. Until or unless both hearts are mutually open and receptive, intimacy remains elusive.

The pursuit of intimacy with God involves complete transparency. We cannot approach Him with one or more tender areas of life remaining off limits. Safeguarding a few hidden corners of our hearts from Him is similar to keeping an active online dating profile after getting married. Such just-in-case hesitancy or keeping-my-options-open perspective don't work in personal or romantic relationships and they surely don't work with God. He desires "truth in the inward parts" and "in the hidden part" He makes us know wisdom (Psalm 51:6). Above all, He deserves and expects complete honesty and openness.

Why are we reluctant to be fully transparent with God? We only defeat ourselves with attempts at secrecy or less than full disclosure with Him. After all, He is omniscient and knows us better than we know ourselves. Any reluctance may have its roots in past pain, past failure, past negative interactions with people, or a lack of full commitment. It could also be due to a lack of trust. To protect ourselves, we erect inner walls under the guise of "guarding our hearts." Yet, in reality, we forget who God really is, ignore His unchanging character, overlook His love, and refuse His divine healing. Unintentionally, our guardedness only closes us off from deeper intimacy with Him. As the adage states: honesty is the best policy. Honesty is also the foundation of relationships.

As the Master Healer, God awaits the hurting places and tattered pieces of our lives. But He won't heal what isn't surrendered to Him. Imagine how much deeper an intimate relationship with Him becomes by allowing Him to heal the past, change current mindsets, and strengthen future commitment to and reliance on Him.

Overlooking God's Promises, Blessings, Favor, and Interaction

Whoever has been forgiven much, loves much (Luke 7:47). Whoever has been blessed and favored much also loves much. Thankful hearts don't take each other for granted. Instead, they remember the good, forgive the bad, and reconcile as soon as possible.

As recipients of mutual blessings and favor, two people in a relationship are grateful for each other. Though they have their differences and maybe even heated discussions, they still look beyond their struggles and remember the good. If all they did was begrudge each other and remember the bad, the relationship would be strained at best. How can true, heartfelt, soul-stirring intimacy exist in that environment?

The reality is God has immensely blessed each person. Of course, individual circumstances won't always be utopian according to human logic. Nor does God grant each person his or her immediate heart's desires all the time. Yet He blesses each person with life, His love and grace, His undeserved mercy, and countless other blessings every day. "Blessed *be* the Lord, *Who* daily loads us *with benefits*, the God of our salvation!" (Psalm 68:19). "Nevertheless He did not leave Himself without witness, in that He did good, gave us rain from heaven and fruitful seasons, filling our hearts with food and gladness" (Acts 14:17)

Limitless benefits, blessings, and favor pour from Him each day. The air we breathe. The constant rhythm of our heartbeats. Even gravity is a blessing that keeps us from floating off into infinite and unforgiving space. As hard as it may be to believe or understand, even adversity is appointed by God (Ecclesiastes 7:14) and can be a blessing in disguise (Psalm 119:71). The practice of emphasizing blessings and favor tends to draw two people closer together. "Bless the LORD, O my soul, and forget not all His benefits" (Psalm 103:2).

When we lack gratitude for what God has done—even His loving discipline (Hebrews 12:6)—our intimacy with Him suffers. Only grateful hearts draw near to Him in praise and thanksgiving for all He has done and is doing in our lives. Imagine how much dearer God becomes if we remember all He has *done* for us and from where He has *brought* us. Salvation alone is worth our everlasting praise. Not to mention the ongoing transformation He performs to conform us into Christlikeness (Romans 8:29). Just remembering all His promises, blessings, and favor should motivate a deeper, closer, more intimate walk with Him.

Lies, Wrong Mindsets, and False Imaginations

Trust is a basic element of any successful relationship. Elements of trust include honesty, openness, and truth. If one person in a relationship discovers the other person believes something false or habitually tries to deceive, then trust erodes like the sand with each ocean wave.

Trust and deception cannot coexist.

Where harmful mindsets exist, cohesion, commonality, and compatibility cannot exist. If a woman's self-image is skewed, her perception of how her boyfriend or husband sees her is also altered—and misaligned with truth. If a man has an inflated ego, he typically won't seek his girlfriend or wife's best interests. If either person constantly suspects the other, there is a high probability that trust and intimacy won't ever exist. Lies, wrong mindsets, and false imaginations are all destructive to relationships. Relational health comes only through truth and healing. Interestingly enough, both truth and healing come from God; therefore, God must be a part of each relationship to reach its maximum potential.

As a loving God who personally created and intimately cares for each person, He sees us truthfully. He doesn't view us through the lens of the lies we believe, the hardened mindsets we maintain, or the false imaginations running rampant in our minds. He sees us through the destiny and purpose for which He created us. In His omniscience, He sees us as who we can become through His redeeming and transforming process. He sees us at our highest and best potential.

Imagine how much more intimate we become with God by seeing ourselves through His eyes—through the revealed, absolute truth of His Word. If only we would accept and trust what He says and stop discounting it. For example, when He says, "I will never leave you nor forsake you" (Hebrews 13:5), we must believe we are always in His presence. When we read, "The Spirit Himself bears witness with our spirit that we are children of God, and if children, then heirs—heirs of God and joint heirs with Christ" (Romans 8:16-17), we must never doubt it. Let's believe it and walk in that truth. Let's act like our Father. Let's mature ourselves in the faith to be reliable heirs of all He has to give. Instead of moping around about things of this life, may we live in such a way as to demonstrate our joint inheritance with Christ in the life to come. Imagine how much different our earthly lives would be if we truly believed we are citizens of heaven (Philippians 3:30) and kings and priests before God (Revelation 1:6). God's Word is full of promises for, and descriptions of, those who are in a personal relationship with Him and who follow Him. He placed it all in His love letter for us to discover and fully accept.

Keep in mind, we have an unrelenting Enemy who will do everything in his power to keep us from walking in the freedom we have in Christ and from accepting who we are in Him. Satan uses our doubt, reluctance, discount programs, and depreciating mindsets to keep us in bondage. He hisses, "You aren't worthy," because he knows the opposite is the truth. He spews, "You're a failure" when he knows we are "more than conquerors" through Him who loves us and gave Himself for us (Romans 8:37). He knows and attacks such critical elements in his attempts to keep us from closer fellowship and strength with God. To help us win this battle, God instructs us to, "Submit to God. Resist the devil and he will flee from you" (James 4:7). Instead of promoting the Devil's lies, wrong mindsets, and false imaginations, let's accept God's absolute truth and see ourselves through God's loving eyes.

Chapter 7

The Battle for the Mind

It is here we must acknowledge the ferocious battle for the human mind. In addition to our aggressive spiritual enemy, the Devil and his wicked imps, our own mindsets contribute to this battle. Romans 8:5-6 explains the opposing sides on this battlefield:

> *For those who live according to the flesh set their minds on the things of the flesh, but those who live according to the Spirit, the things of the Spirit. For to be carnally minded is death, but to be spiritually minded is life and peace.*

The implication of "set their minds" indicates personal choice. We choose our thoughts, perceptions, mindsets, fantasies, meditations, prejudices, and agendas. We can choose to have *carnal* minds or *spiritual* minds. It all depends on what we choose to think—the mindsets we choose to maintain. We can continue believing what may be comfortable or sensible to us, although contrary to God's Word. Or we can surrender our mindsets to God, bring every thought captive to the obedience of Christ (2 Corinthians 10:5), and think about what aligns with God's Word. A godly way of thinking involves "whatever things are true … noble … just … pure … lovely… of good report; if there is any virtue and if there is anything praiseworthy—meditate on these things" (Philippians 4:8). We can sway the tide of battle by choosing the correct mindset.

The apostle Paul further described the battlefield, the weapons, and the war strategy to show us how we develop and live with victorious, God-honoring, and scripturally aligned mindsets.

For the weapons of our warfare are not carnal but mighty in God for pulling down strongholds, casting down arguments and every high thing that exalts itself against the knowledge of God, bringing every thought into captivity to the obedience of Christ (2 Corinthians 10:4-5).

Wow! These verses hold so much vital information to spiritual success and intimacy with God. To glean the harvest of truth in these verses, let's break down some key words and concepts.

- **Weapons** – These are offensive, not defensive, instruments of war. They imply deliberate intentionality of taking the war to the Enemy and require that we know when and how to use them. We find additional descriptions of these weapons as part of the armor of God in Ephesians 6:10-18.

- **Warfare** – This involves military service along with the associated danger. The Christian walk, as well as intimacy with God, involves serious, strategic engagement. As followers of Jesus Christ, the call to spiritual warfare has one ultimate goal: to please Him who enlisted us as soldiers (2 Timothy 2:4).

- **Mighty** – Our weapons are powerful and sufficient for the task. But they are mighty only through God, not in our own strength. "I can do all things through Christ who strengthens me" (Philippians 4:13). The weapons provide all the power we need for victory, yet we are wise to learn how to use them—and practice using them every day.

- **Pulling / Casting Down** – These words describe demolishing or destroying with violence. They suggest an intense, deliberate, passionate desire to change. In light of the context, they refer to an aggressive, deliberate mental reboot, so to speak. The same Greek word is used in Acts 13:19 to describe the military destruction of seven nations by the Israelites when they victoriously took possession of the Promised Land God gave them. No surrender. No prisoners. No unclaimed land.

- **Stronghold** – A fortified or well-defended place. It refers to any stubborn mindsets, opinions, or agendas we hold dear for any reason. Any such stronghold that conflicts with God's Word must be instantly and aggressively rejected and demolished, then replaced with the mindset of Christ Jesus (Philippians 2:5).

- **Argument** – This refers to imaginations or reasonings. It includes all the perceptions we've built up over time as our reality—even our preferential reality or what has now become known as each person's "inner truth." No matter how much we cherish our favored arguments, all of them that contradict God's Word must be immediately considered false and subsequently abandoned. It bears repeating—*all of them*. To find and maintain intimacy with God, we must, "lay aside every weight, and the sin which so easily ensnares" (Hebrews 12:1) which includes our faulty mindsets.

- **High Thing** – An elevated place, thing, or obstacle. This is whatever we enthrone in our minds as comfortable fact. We all see what we want to see based on our experiences. If our loved ones drive certain models of cars, we notice those cars everywhere. This is because we've elevated those specific cars in our minds and programmed ourselves to see them in hopes of seeing our loved ones. Anything or anyone occupying a higher priority than the "knowledge of God"—all obstacles that hinder intimacy with God—must be surrendered to Him. Until God is Lord *of* all, He isn't Lord *at* all. There is no such thing as partial lordship—or partial intimacy.

- **Thought** – This includes perception, purpose, intellect, disposition, and mindset. Whatever is left after pulling down strongholds, arguments, and high things is included here. As a final sweep, it includes whatever remains hidden in the secret, protected recesses of our minds. This is where we ask God for words and meditations that are acceptable to Him and aligned with His Word (Psalm 19:14). To help in this endeavor, we pray, "Search me, O God, and know my heart; try me, and know my anxieties; and see if *there is any* wicked way in me, and lead me in the way everlasting." (Psalm 139:23-24)

- **Captivity** – This implies leading away as a captive or being imprisoned. It describes the intentional willingness to capture all normal, previous thoughts and force the mind to think differently. When a thought enters the mind that contradicts what God says, we assault it immediately and lead it away captive. We don't pamper, nurture, or allow it to roam freely as it previously did. Once we imprison such thoughts, prison breaks are strictly forbidden. Even those stray thoughts that wander off when praying or spending time with God must be recognized, captured, and redirected. Paul describes this battle in Romans 7:15-25. Either we allow sin to hold us captive or we take it captive through the power of Jesus Christ and the influence of the Holy Spirit.

- **Obedience** – Attentive listening, compliance, and submission. This is the crucial point of the battle over the mind. "Do you not know that to whom you present yourselves slaves to obey, you are that one's slaves whom you obey, whether of sin leading to death, or of obedience leading to righteousness?"(Romans 6:16). When we justify and excuse our preferential thoughts, imaginations, fantasies, perceptions, and mindsets, we embrace the Enemy and continue struggling with his mental attacks. On the contrary, we experience victory only by surrendering all thoughts to the obedience of Christ. How do we do this? By immediately recognizing and confronting any sinful thought, binding it up, carrying it to the foot of the cross of Calvary, allowing the precious blood of Jesus to drench it, and then proclaiming, "Stay there until Jesus allows you to leave!"

As we've already seen, the apostle Paul presented the personal choice to be either spiritually or carnally minded. The resulting lifestyle depends on this mental choice—the fruit reveals the root. The apostle James warns that a double-minded person is unstable in all his ways (James 1:8). A person's mindset overflows into every aspect of his or her life. Jesus explained that what is in a person's heart eventually comes out (Luke 6:44-45). If we fill our hearts and minds with Jesus, He will bleed out and saturate our spiritual battlefield, giving us the victory.

The battle for the mind is a difficult, savage, and ongoing struggle. Satan targeted Adam and Eve's minds to induce them to question what God said. He also assaulted Jesus by misquoting Scripture—all of which Jesus confronted with, "It is written…" The battle for the mind is where Satan engages his most successful attacks. However, we have the weapons, strategy, and choice to recognize and repel his assaults by willfully and forcibly aligning our mindsets with God's Word. Spending quality time in His Word and presence not only strengthens us in this battle, it also promotes deeper intimacy with Him.

Joseph L. Hall (1868) quite beautifully described the sweet interaction, communion, and presence when sitting at the feet of Jesus.

> Sitting at the feet of Jesus,
> Oh, what words I hear Him say!
> Happy place! so near, so precious!
> May it find me there each day.
>
> Sitting at the feet of Jesus,
> There I love to weep and pray;
> While I from His fullness gather
> Grace and comfort every day.

Bless me, O my Savior, bless me,
As I'm waiting at Thy feet;
Oh, look down in love upon me,
Let me see Thy face so sweet.

Give me, Lord, the mind of Jesus,
Keep me holy as He is;
May I prove I've been with Jesus,
Who is all my righteousness.[3]

Chapter 8

Past Spiritual Failure Does Not Dictate
Future Spiritual Success

One unique obstacle to intimacy with God deserves a specific callout: past spiritual failure. Although it is part of the battle for the mind, it needs special attention. Its subtle attack undermines peace of mind and hamstrings any attempts at current spiritual success. By its very nature, it becomes a self-fulfilling, self-defeating prophecy.

Unfortunately, many people struggle with past spiritual failure. They think, *I've failed God so miserably in my past, I seriously doubt He wants anything to do with me now.* Or even worse, *I've tried everything I know to do and still haven't found, nor do I enjoy, a sense of sweet fellowship with God.* Such mindsets of guilt, failure, despair, and hopelessness are unfortunate and unpleasant indeed—and completely unnecessary. Instead of ushering us into the sweet and tender presence of our loving Father, such mindsets imprison us in the pigpen of the prodigal far-off country. Even the nearby countries of comfort and complacency steal our spiritual contentment.

It is truly a tragedy to feel disconnected from the One who loves us, died for us, desires a personal relationship with us, and wants to spend eternity with us. But here is a concrete truth that is a first step in overcoming this obstacle: barriers to intimacy aren't God's fault. He is who He is and has done everything necessary to initiate and establish an intimate, thriving relationship with us. In addition to giving us His Word and sending His Son, He gave us free will, liberty, and the choice to join Him on the journey. In the story of the prodigal son (Luke 15:11-24), the distance between the father and son, as well as the disconnectedness of their fellowship, were not the father's fault. He hadn't abandoned the relationship. Not until the wayward son *chose to return* to His father did the distance and disconnectedness vanish.

King David provides further evidence that past spiritual failure doesn't dictate future spiritual success. His abysmal failures in the adultery with Bathsheba and murder of Uriah qualified him as a prime candidate for future failure. Yet after his repentance and remorse (Psalm 51), he was called a man after God's own heart (Acts 13:22). Only the intimacy of relationship and fellowship in God's presence enables such reconciliation and restoration.

One of the often-overlooked rewards of spending time in God's presence is the renewal—the quickening—He gives. Consider the story of Aaron's rod that budded (Numbers 17:1-8). Some of the Israelites challenged Aaron's authority as high priest. In obedience to God, Moses asked each tribal leader to give him their walking staffs. He then placed them all, along with Aaron's, in the Tabernacle before God and awaited His response. After spending one night in God's presence, Aaron's dead, dry walking stick actually budded, blossomed, and yielded new almonds. One night in God's presence—one touch from God's quickening Spirit—revitalized new life to what was previously dead and dry.

One night.

One renewing, restoring touch from God.

That is just one reward of drawing near and spending time in God's life-infusing, light-shining, liberty-bestowing presence. He can revitalize our deadness of soul, our dryness from this world. He is waiting for us and has the renewing power to enable victorious lives and sweeter intimacy with Him. But He leaves the choice to us. We choose to walk in new victory or stumble in past defeat.

Pulling this all together, we arrive at one conclusion. Each person gets as close to God as he or she chooses. Better yet, each person gets as close to God as he or she *desires*. Everyone has the freewill choice to believe God, to trust His Word, and to apply what He says to their lives. But there is also the matter of the heart's desire—valued priority and unbridled passion. We must want intimacy with God more than anything else—yes, more than the bondage of past defeats. "I spread out my hands to You; my soul longs for You like a thirsty land" (Psalm 143:6).

Scripture tells us God meets those who passionately seek Him—now, in the present, regardless of the past. Those who "hunger and thirst for righteousness" will be filled (Matthew 5:6). Whoever believes on Jesus will "never thirst" (John 6:35). God rewards those who "diligently seek Him" (Hebrews 11:6). Once we make the choice for a relationship with God, there is also a deep, diligent, passionate desire for closeness to Him. And He promises to meet that desire with Himself. The awesome news is His promises are not conditional to only those who have never experienced spiritual defeat. His mercy and compassion, available to everyone, are renewed every morning (Lamentations 3:22-23).

Unlike human relationships, where mutual love and intimacy vary depending on both individual's interest and commitment, intimacy with God is strictly dependent on us. We do not have to speculate on God's love, interest, or commitment toward us. Even a child with limited Bible knowledge understands, "For God so loved the world that He gave His only begotten Son, that whoever believes in Him should not perish but have everlasting life" (John 3:16). The apostle John, also known as "the Beloved," exclaimed, "Behold what manner of love the Father has bestowed on us, that we should be called children of God!" (1 John 3:1). God's love is constant, unconditional, and everlasting because He *is* love (1 John 4:8). When pursuing intimacy with God, never question His love or His desire to welcome you into His loving embrace.

Additionally, human relationships sometimes require mutually working through intimacy issues. But God has no "uh-oh" moments nor does He have to work through any issues. As omniscient, He never thinks, "*I didn't know that about you, I didn't know you would react that way*, or *I didn't know you felt that way*. As immutable, He cannot change or compromise to accommodate how we feel or what we think. He is who He is and will continue being who He is—loving, just, merciful, gracious, patient, and holy, among many other characteristics. Any working-through-issues falls completely on us.

God is who He is and has completely accomplished everything we need to begin and maintain an intimate relationship with Him. He chose us even before He created the universe (Ephesians 1:4). He sent Jesus to die in our place to remove the barrier of sin that prevents an intimate relationship with Him. He gave us His Word to inform us and His Spirit to transform us. Only through Him can we understand how to enter, maintain, and enjoy intimate relationship and fellowship with Him. He can do no more than what He has already done. Once we understand this, we quickly realize that any obstacles we encounter in the pursuit of intimacy with God are ours to discover and resolve.

God remains forever consistent with His essence (Malachi 3:6). He loves everyone because He is love (1 John 4:8). He is incapable of showing partiality (Acts 10:34). He keeps His promises and is unable to lie (Hebrews 6:18). He promises to hear our prayers and respond (Matthew 6:6). Humans, on the other hand, are rather inconsistent and fickle, often changing mindsets, priorities, and passions without reason or warning. As sad as it is to admit, we treat others unequally and partially depending on our personal preferences, biases, and expected benefits in return. But God has no such relational barriers.

Even when we think we've tried everything to rest in His presence and it doesn't *feel* like He is there, we must have faith that He is. Just because He is silent doesn't mean He is absent. When we cannot see His hand or feel His closeness, we must accept His Word and trust His heart. Job experienced a whirlwind of disasters and questioned his very existence. Yet through it all, he never lost faith in the One who loved Him. "Though He slay me, yet will I trust Him" (Job 13:15). Regardless of our feelings, current circumstances, heartaches, or adversity, we can trust our heavenly Father's love, sovereign control, and unique purpose.

Establishing and enjoying tender closeness with God requires moving beyond past failed attempts. But we must get our eyes off ourselves and keep them firmly fixed on Jesus, the author and finisher of our faith (Hebrews 12:2). Whatever didn't work in the past, we must identify the contributing reasons and then move on. If we haven't yet identified the remaining obstacle that hinders deeper intimacy with God, let's keep opening up to Him in full transparency, then surrendering whatever He brings to light. It is important to let go of the past. Whatever God brings to mind, surrender it immediately. Keep taking one step at a time, trusting Him to reward your faith, diligence, passion and desire. "Being confident of this very thing, that He who has begun a good work in you will complete *it* until the day of Jesus Christ" (Philippians 1:6).

Keep in mind, Satan will do whatever possible to restrict or disturb intimacy with God. Resist him. Do not listen to his rubbish about past failures. If you have repented, past failures are under the blood of Calvary. Forgive yourself—God has already forgiven you. Fight against yourself and any self-imposed barriers to spiritual intimacy. Draw near to God— He has already promised to draw near to you (James 4:8). Trust Him to do just that every time you enter His presence.

Chapter 9

Steps to Establishing Intimacy with God

Successful, fulfilling human relationships involve communication, companionship, connection, collaboration, and commonalities—all of which develop trust and ever-deepening intimacy. In the relationship with God, He *communicates* with us through His Word and Spirit. He is the *Companion* who sticks closer than a brother (Proverbs 18:24). As our sovereign Creator and Redeemer, He *connects* with us on many levels. He is reliable and may be trusted implicitly. In His great love for us, He longs for intimacy with each person. Once we open our hearts to deeper intimacy with Him, He *collaborates* with us to transform us and our relationship with Him. As we grow more intimate and spiritually mature, we find numerous *commonalities* with Him.

How can we make or choose to allow this to happen?

As with human relationships, there must be a beginning before ongoing development. A deeper connection is impossible without a relationship. Falling in love is the beginning; staying in love is the ongoing journey toward deeper intimacy.

Beginning the Relationship

Did you ever know someone who was in a relationship that crashed and burned because one person presumed a closer level of intimacy than the other? For sake of clarity, let's imagine such a relationship between Bob and Jane. In Jane's mind, she pictured the relationship going the distance because she presumed what she was enjoying was the real deal. She picked out her wedding dress in a bridal magazine, made a list of bridesmaids, and started researching wedding venues. Meanwhile, Bob was enjoying the convenience and comfort of their companionship. He enjoyed Jane's company and the many activities they did together. But when Jane revealed her long-term vision, Bob was highly confused. Having never considered what they enjoyed as a *relationship*, he eventually told Jane, "Let's just be friends." Dumbfounded and heartbroken, Jane asked why the sudden change of mind. Bob clarified, "It's not a sudden change of mind. I just don't see us as more than good friends who are having a great time together."

Ouch.

Sadly, the same scenario happens in relationships with God. Many people presume they are in a relationship with Him when, in fact, they are not. They base their presumption on religious beliefs, church denomination, good works, charitable donations, the happy feeling they get when singing worship songs, and the fact they were born in Christian homes. The reasons are endless.

Bottom line, they enjoy spiritual dating but are not in a relationship with God.

Jesus confirmed this when He said, "Not everyone who says to Me, 'Lord, Lord,' shall enter the kingdom of heaven... Many will say to Me in that day, 'Lord, Lord, have we not prophesied in Your name, cast out demons in Your name, and done many wonders in Your name?' And then I will declare to them, 'I never knew you; depart from Me'" (Matthew 7:21-23). It is critically and eternally important to establish a relationship with God in only the way He recognizes.

Which brings us to the second consideration about relationships. Casual friendship or knowing *about* someone isn't the same as an exclusive, intimate relationship. Friends can be buddies, pals, friends for life, even friends who know each other's deepest, darkest secrets. Occasionally people do marry their best friends. But when we are talking about an intimate relationship with God, simply being friendly with "the Man upstairs" isn't enough to qualify as a relationship. Additionally, some friendships evolve naturally over time, yet with no commitment of exclusivity or intimacy. But a relationship with God doesn't begin or progress like that. Why? Because, "The natural man (outside of a relationship with God) does not receive the things of the Spirit of God, for they are foolishness to him; nor can he know them, because they are spiritually discerned" (1 Corinthians 2:14, parenthesis added). There is nothing casual or evolutionary about the beginning of a relationship with God. It is a specific, spiritual event just as a newborn baby has a specific event at delivery.

God is very precise about how to enter into an intimate relationship with Him. Jesus summarized it by saying, "I am the way, the truth, and the life. No one comes to the Father except through Me" (John 14:6). Only through faith in Jesus Christ can we have an intimate relationship with God. This process of faith is called salvation—being born again, born from above, reborn spiritually and supernaturally.

Why do we need this?

Because Adam's disobedience in the Garden of Eden severed intimate fellowship with God. As descendants of Adam, this sin nature was passed along to each person (Romans 5:12). Subsequently, the penalty for sin is eternal separation from God in hell (Romans 6:23). Thankfully, Jesus died in our place (Isaiah 53:4-6) so He could offer us eternal life through His death and resurrection (John 3:16). By claiming and appropriating His sacrifice as our own, and accepting Him as our Lord and Savior, we have a restored relationship with God (Romans 5:1-2).

When Jesus talked with Nicodemus, He explained a person must be born "from above" (John 3:3-7). This is the new birth whereby a person's spirit, previously dead and deformed by sin, is reborn. This miraculous event takes place when God's Holy Spirit enters our hearts, reviving us spiritually, and living within us (Romans 8:9-11). We initiate this relationship by genuinely confessing Jesus Christ as Lord and fully believing He rose from the dead (Romans 10:9-10).

God honors this step of faith by giving us Himself. He gives us faith-inducing, faith-building, faith-sustaining promises in His Word (2 Peter 1:4). God's Word is our instructional guide to get to know Him better while also learning how to live the Christian life. God also gives us the Holy Spirit to live inside us (John 14:16-17). The Spirit's role is to guide us into God's absolute truth (John 16:13-14) and empower us to walk in this new life (Romans 6:4). We have two eternal, unchanging, reliable sources—God's Word and God's Spirit—right from the beginning of the relationship. These are also the spiritual aids to guide us into His presence.

Developing the Relationship

Upon entering a relationship, ongoing honesty and transparency are crucial for the relationship to grow deeper and for intimacy to flourish. Mutual connection depends on openness and vulnerability. Any hidden agendas, selfish motives, and secrets are poisonous to trust and eventually destroy the relationship. If any such negative traits exist, even though a relationship continues, the blossom of intimacy will quickly fade. Until such time as both people are completely open and honest, the relationship remains veiled in the shadows of mistrust and the dullness of superficiality.

Similarly, overcoming obstacles to spiritual intimacy involves honest self-examination and confession of whatever the Holy Spirit reveals. God helps us understand how sin breaks down communion and fellowship with Him. "If I regard iniquity in my heart, the Lord will not hear" (Psalm 66:18). The Israelites found this out the hard way. "We have transgressed and rebelled; You have not pardoned. You have covered Yourself with a cloud, that prayer should not pass through" (Lamentations 3:42, 44). Yet when we come before God with complete openness of heart and immediate repentance and surrender, we reignite the relational warmth with Him. "Let us draw near with a true heart in full assurance of faith, having our hearts sprinkled from an evil conscience." (Hebrews 10:22).

A successful relationship should expect and encourage honest communication. Obviously, it is easy to express tender, loving thoughts and feelings. But we should also be able to share (civilly) our frustrations, anger, disappointments, and other negative expressions that are part of the human experience. The relationship with God is no different. He can handle our frustrations, impatience, anger, discouragement, disappointments, grief, and all other negative sentiments. He already knows what we're feeling and thinking, so we may as well be honest with Him and not try to hide or keep anything bottled up. That doesn't work well with human relationships and surely doesn't work with God. Actually, He expects and deserves our honesty at all times. When we are honest, transparent, and vulnerable, He then reveals more of Himself and takes us deeper with Him.

As an example, consider another analogy from the story of the prodigal son (Luke 15:11-24). When that young man chose to leave his father, their fellowship was severed. The relationship remained intact, but there was no longer any warmth of personal interaction or communication. As God so often does with us, that father didn't interfere in his son's rebellious journey. Nor did he check on him or even visit him in the pigpen of his sin. The father stayed true to himself, his position, and his place. Only when the son repented, surrendered his will, and returned to his father was their relational intimacy restored.

There will be times in every believer's life when fellowship with God is hindered or, at the very least, not as intense as it once was. Invariably, life happens and quality time alone with God gets de-prioritized to a hurried prayer as we rush about our daily responsibilities. Our passion cools. We take God for granted. Sadly, even God's faithful blessings sometime induce us to grow spiritually complacent and lazy. Mere existence replaces thriving intimacy. This is where self-examination comes into play. As with personal relationships, a periodic inventory is necessary. *Am I as close with God as I can be? Better yet, am I as close with Him as He wants me to be? What can I do to reignite my passion with God? What prevents me from drawing nearer to Him?*

Maintaining the Relationship

Communication is critical in a relationship, but each person has a different communication style. With this added dimension of complexity, something as seemingly easy as sharing and receiving verbal messages gets garbled. Learning and adapting to each other's style helps us communicate clearly. But the important thing is that we listen and express honest, vulnerable thoughts with each other.

Thankfully, God understands and uses all communication styles. We don't need to be afraid of stumbling through our thoughts, not saying things the right way, or Him not understanding us. He knows our thoughts and motives. We can approach Him confidently (Hebrews 4:16) about whatever is on our hearts and minds. With God, this method of communication involves prayer.

For some people, praying is easy. For others, some instructional help may be necessary. There are several components of prayer we can easily remember with the ACTS prayer formula:[4]

- *Adoration* – time spent praising God for who He *is*, not necessarily for what He has *done* or is *doing* for us.

- *Confession* – the admission and repentance of sin; seeing sin from God's perspective.

- *Thanksgiving* – the expression of gratitude for God's many blessings and favor.

- *Supplication* – offering our requests, petitions, and intercession.

We start with praise and end with requests. What a great communication secret for personal relationships as well. Requests are usually better received when they are preceded by praise. A great source of praises to God would be reading aloud through the Psalms during regularly scheduled quiet times. Even when circumstances are less than ideal, we have much for which to praise Him. Praising God helps prepare our hearts to share our requests.

The progression in intimacy with God also includes releasing the unknown. This happens when we surrender control over all the indefinite, uncontrollable events of life. We willingly yield them to God's sovereign orchestration, trusting Him to work all things for our good and His glory. Here again, this level of mature trust usually doesn't happen immediately. It is difficult and scary to release into God's hands something or someone near and dear to our hearts. But we develop the willingness and ability to do so by spending quality time with Him and by expressing honest vulnerability about our fears and our need for increasing faith. How much easier it becomes when we realize He is already in control of everything.

The difficulty usually arises in our hesitancy to surrender to His perfect will.

As an additional step in nurturing our relationship with God, the apostle Peter encourages followers of Jesus to "grow in the grace and knowledge of our Lord and Savior Jesus Christ" (2 Peter 3:18). Growth usually involves change; change usually involves growing pains. Growing in grace means we develop strength and maturity in our Christian walk. Our trust in God deepens. Our dependence on Him increases. We spend increasing time in His Word. We acknowledge the Lordship-servant interaction—what He says, we do. We are increasingly grateful for His sacrifice as our Savior. We also share our faith with others so they may begin a relationship with Him. Ultimately, growing in grace and knowledge of Him involves spending quality time in His presence.

There is an interesting correlation at this level. The more we grow and mature in our Christian walk and fellowship with Him, He may answer us less. As an example, a newborn baby gets immediate and constant attention. He cannot care for himself, so his parents are attentive to his cries, needs, and safety. But as the baby grows, the urgent attention decreases. A mother or father still loves their teenage or adult son or daughter but they expect him or her to mature to a place of self-sufficiency. With God, this won't be self-sufficiency so much as it is developing the faith and trust in Him to sovereignly act to His divine purpose—even when we don't like, understand, or even see it. Although time in His presence is still incredibly sweet and empowering, His seeming unresponsiveness may correlate with our increasing trust and maturity. Again, just because God is silent doesn't mean He is absent. He is always there, sovereignly orchestrating people and events behind the scenes to our good and His ultimate purpose.

When driving his family on a road trip, a father may not respond to every, "are we there yet?" from his children. He knows the way and is capable of bringing them all safely to their destination on time. For this reason, we bring our heart's desires to our heavenly Father with the stipulation, "Not my will, Father, but Your will be done, Your way, and according to Your schedule." Such trust and surrender are pinnacles of intimacy with Him.

Chapter 10

Discovering Four Levels of Intimacy with God

Intimacy with God isn't an all-or-nothing reality. There is a maturing progression of nearness with Him. We shouldn't expect to immediately enjoy the deepest levels of intimacy of a relationship by simply wanting it. Nor should we expect to spend precious moments with God without devotedly and passionately seeking them.

As we've seen, intimacy takes time, vulnerability, and devoted passion. In human relationships, each new day involves the choice to get to know each other better, to love each other deeper, to interact with each other on a closer level. As time passes and passion grows, people in relationships achieve new levels of discovery. The more time spent together, the more they get to know each other. The more they know and become known, the more trusting and intimate their relationship grows.

This same principle applies to spiritual intimacy. Various Scripture references reveal at least four different levels of fellowship or intimacy with Christ. Although our *relationship* with Him may be secure, our *fellowship* varies due to several contributing factors. The following diagram describes the levels, the people groups or individuals in each level, and the underlying motives of each level. As the side arrows indicate, our intimacy with God isn't constant. It moves either closer or more distant depending on our choices. Sometimes our passion for closeness to God burns hot; other times it cools as we drift from Him.

Beginning with the largest group, let's look at each one in progression toward the deepest level of intimacy with God.

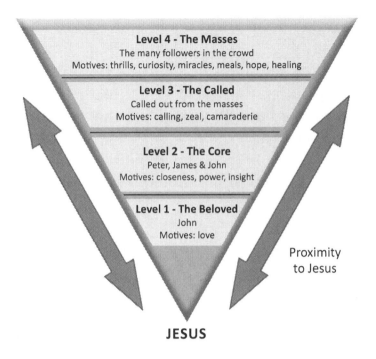

JESUS

Level 4 – The Masses

This largest group represents the mass of humanity—believers and unbelievers alike. Through various genres and venues, almost everyone has heard something about Jesus. Missionaries travel to far-off lands with the gospel. Bibles have been translated into numerous languages and regional dialects. Television, radio, and online outlets proclaim the good news of Jesus Christ. Various forms of social media contain nonstop streams of personal testimonies or religious content.

And yet not everyone responds the same way to the message. Some believe; many do not. They may not know, hear, or understand every specific detail, but they are at least within earshot of the story of Jesus.

In Jesus' day, the general public heard and followed Him. His teachings attracted the masses—even those who opposed Him. Their motives for following were varied. Some were curious while others were deeply interested in what He had to say. Religious people grew increasingly irritated with His message and actions. *Who does He think He is?* Upon hearing and seeing Jesus' healings, many people arrived hoping to be similarly healed. Or they brought their sick friends for healing. There was also the thrill of His miracles. *Who doesn't enjoy a magic show?* He also raised several people from the dead. Then there were those who followed Him for the free food. *Why not follow Him?* Regardless of the reasons or the motives of their hearts, this largest group had at least a superficial interaction with Jesus.

In current day application, many people have heard *about* Jesus. Millions attend church, read His Word, and claim some knowledge about Him. Some in this group are new believers starting their journey of intimacy with God by having placed their trust in Jesus as Savior and Lord. Others may be longer-term believers, yet they don't make the effort to deepen their relationship or grow more intimate with God. They seem satisfied to remain in the shallow waters of immature faith with no real sense of His active presence in their lives (Hebrews 5:12-13). To that extent, intimacy in God's embrace is a foreign concept they have heard about but not desired or pursued. Without daily doses of His Word, they remain oblivious to the deeper, more abundant life He offers (John 10:10).

Level 3 – The Called

For the most part, this level represents those who have heard about Jesus and have come into relationship with Him. They have placed their trust in Him as Savior and Lord and have chosen to believe His Word and apply it to their lives. They may serve in their local churches, sing in the choirs, volunteer for mission trips, or participate in some form of spiritual service. But this group also includes unbelievers who play the part or who haven't genuinely entered into a personal, intimate relationship with Christ. As Judas Iscariot, the impostor and betrayer, there may be some in this group who hear and see what should draw them closer to God, yet they remain distant.

From the masses, Jesus called the twelve disciples to follow Him. These men came from all walks of life and different societal levels. Some were uneducated, others were employees of Rome. One denied Him, another betrayed Him. They all forsook Him after His arrest and one doubted Him after His resurrection. Yet this group was closer than the masses. They heard Him more clearly, saw His miracles more closely. Apart from the crowd, they had occasion to interact personally with Him on a regular basis.

This level of intimacy seems to incorporate most believers. They are in relationship with Him and enjoy a consistent level of closeness with Him. They serve Him regularly and may even spend regular quiet time in His presence. Their motives tend to include the excitement of the relationship, the fellowship with other believers, and the security of an eternity with God in heaven. If there were no deeper intimacy, most would be content to stay at this level.

But as we find in human relationships, the heart cries for a deeper connectedness, a more profound sense of nearness. We have been made in the image of God—at the core of our being is a God-shaped vacuum. Even though He fills it through salvation, there remains the compelling desire to "know Him who is true; and we are in Him who is true, in His Son Jesus Christ" (1 John 5:20). Our inner calling is to conform more and more each day to Christlikeness (Romans 8:29). Usually in life, what isn't growing is stagnating or dying.

Level 2 – The Core

This level introduces yet a nearer fellowship with God. This group, even smaller, includes those who seek a much closer walk with God than most others do. They sense the Holy Spirit nudging them. They maintain consistent quiet times with God. Their lives display Christlikeness. Many believers wistfully desire to be part of this group—yet few are committed to the effort and sacrifice it requires.

Peter, James, and John comprised the core group whom Jesus took into confidence on several occasions. They saw miracles the other disciples didn't see (Luke 8:51) and got to ask Him questions in private (Mark 13:3). These three also saw His glory on the Mount of Transfiguration

(Matthew 17:1-13) and were invited to go further with Him in the Garden of Gethsemane (Mark 14:32-33). Two members of this group, James and John, were bold enough to ask Jesus if they could sit on His right and left hands in His kingdom (Mark 10:35-37). Jesus responded by asking if they would "drink of the cup" required of such a request. Meaning, there is a price to pay for this level of intimacy with God.

Believers at this level of intimacy desire close proximity with Him. They seek to be filled with His power and endowed with His insight. Every activity of every day is a new opportunity to engage with Him. They actively seek to grow deeper in their relationship and allow His transformation "until Christ is formed" in them (Galatians 4:19). They willingly give of their time and resources to help build and expand His kingdom purposes. Time spent in His presence is a precious treasure, not an obligated ritual. Reading His Word and listening to His Spirit are vital components to their daily routines. They quickly apply spiritual truth (James 1:22) and make deliberate attempts to encourage (not quench) the Holy Spirit's work in their lives (1 Thessalonians 5:19). Quite often, God calls, anoints, and entrusts them with ministry where they can educate, encourage, and equip other believers.

Level 1 – The Beloved

This closest level of intimacy correlates to the apostle John, also known as the Beloved. It was he who leaned against Jesus during the Last Supper (John 21:20). Many commentators believe it was he who followed Christ throughout His arrest in Gethsemane (Mark 14:51-52) and His judgment in Caiaphas' house (John 18:13-16). It was he to whom Jesus entrusted His mother's care (John 19:25-27). John also ran to the empty tomb after the resurrection (John 20:2-4). Intense love fueled John's dedication to his dear Friend, Savior, and Lord. He loved Him in life; he loved him in death. Upon hearing of His resurrection, John was the first to believe it without yet seeing Jesus alive (John 20:8). Near the end of his life, God entrusted John with the Revelation of the end times, Christ's return, His future kingdom, and His future eternity (Revelation 1:1-2).

In reading the gospels and John's epistles, we sense the close relationship he enjoyed with Jesus. From the day of his call to discipleship, we find John always in Jesus' presence. He hung on Jesus' every word. Wanting to be wherever Jesus was, he followed immediately. Listening and watching his Master, through trials and triumphs, gave John a deeper appreciation of God's love in practical action. He heard Jesus say, "By this all will know that you are My disciples, if you have love for one another" (John 13:35) and later echoed that sentiment, "Beloved, let us love one another, for love is of God; and everyone who loves is born of God and knows God. He who does not love does not know God, for God is love" (1 John 4:7-8). He never lost sight of the marvelous, magnanimous love of God. "Behold what manner of love the Father has bestowed on us, that we should be called children of God!" (1 John 3:1). It was John who shared the primary theme of God's love for mankind. "For God so loved the world that He gave His only begotten Son, that whoever believes in Him should not perish but have everlasting life" (John 3:16). No wonder John is referred to as "the disciple Jesus loved" or the Beloved.

This pinnacle of intimacy represents those individuals who snuggle so close to Jesus they can hear His heartbeat. Spending time alone with Him is the highlight of each day. Although fewer in number, they resemble and reflect Christlikeness in all they do. We see Jesus in them. We want what they have—precious peace in God's presence, sweet satisfaction with His Word, and abiding faith no matter the circumstance. Their hearts align with His as they walk daily in the Spirit and enjoy constant enjoyment with Him. Their lives seem to be emblazoned with heaven's holy anointing. Their motto is, "I am my beloved's, and my beloved is mine" (Song of Solomon 6:3).

Oh, to know and be known like this. To love and be loved like this. This should be the crowning joy of every believer and earnest longing of every unbeliever.

Chapter 11

What Determines the Difference Between Intimacy Levels?

Now that we have discovered and described the four levels, several questions arise.

If God isn't partial, why don't more people enjoy the pinnacle of intimacy with God? With the benefits that accompany a close walk with God, why wouldn't each follower of Christ commit to the journey? What makes the difference between those who achieve such intimacy and those who don't? What is the distinguishing characteristic that differentiates each unique level of intimacy?

An even more important set of questions is this: *At what level am I? Do I truly want to go deeper with God? If so, what am I willing to do to achieve it?*

From everything we find in God's Word, it comes down to one thing: individual choice.

It is the God-given freewill choice to choose for or against Him. Finding and maintaining intimacy with God is the personal willingness to establish and foster a consistent, growing, and prioritized level of vulnerable interaction with Him. The more we want to know Him, the more He reveals Himself to us (Hebrews 11:6). The closer we get to Him, the closer He gets to us (James 4:8). Hallelujah! What a Savior, Lord, and Friend.

Admittedly, individual choices are influenced by past experiences, personal temperament, willingness to trust, priorities, and responsibilities. Past experiences may either encourage or restrict our choices depending on what we've tried in the past and the outcomes of those attempts. If we previously tried and failed, we may be skeptical about trying again. With each person's unique temperament comes differing levels of expression and vulnerability. A reclusive introvert may be less expressive and vulnerable than a talkative extrovert. Our willingness to trust depends on past betrayals or loyalty by those we trusted. Priorities may be more worldly focused than they should be. Our responsibilities may be so cumbersome that we may not have time to consider making choices for something different or better. Such is the human experience and the real struggle of devoting ourselves to deeper intimacy with God.

No matter the complexities involved, each person has the choice to come to God, enter a relationship with Him, and foster a deeper level of intimacy. He made each of us; He knows us better than we know ourselves. More importantly, He meets each of us where we are and promises to walk the journey of deeper intimacy together. He stands outside each heart's door knocking, waiting for the invitation to enter. He doesn't force His way in; He acknowledges the only door handle is on the inside. The choice to open the door is ours alone.

But what about other influences that could impact the differences in the intimacy levels? *What about sovereign predestination? What if God does have favorites? Maybe there are unwritten rules that permanently keep each person at each level.*

A review of each issue brings us back to individual choice. There is no escaping the inevitability of personal choice and personal accountability before God (Romans 14:12). One day we will all stand before Him to acknowledge our decision—for or against him.

Predestination?

Some may argue these described levels of intimacy with God are predested. Their premise is that we don't really have any choice in the matter. God, in His sovereignty, has already predestined those who would be saved as well as those at different levels of intimacy with Him. Everything in life proceeds at some foreordained, divine plan, and we are just along for the ride.

It is true that God, who is all-knowing, already understands how each person will exercise his or her free will. But that is foreknowledge, not predestination. Just because an all-knowing God already sees the outcome of individual choice doesn't negate our ability to exercise it fully and freely. Scripture clearly reveals the freewill concept with phrases like "of his own free will" (Leviticus 1:3), "self-will" (Genesis 49:6), "your own will" (Leviticus 22:29), "whoever believes" (John 3:16), and "If anyone desires to come after Me, let him deny himself, and take up his cross, and follow Me" (Matthew 16:24). All these scenarios involve the exercise of individual free will. Just because God foreknows our freewill choices doesn't mean we are destined or forced to make them.

God is timeless and resides in the eternal present tense of I AM (Exodus 3:14). As such, He can relive any moment in time. He is always present. When we make past, present, or future decisions, He is already there and knows the choices and outcomes of those choices. But the fact remains, the choices are ours to make.

Since God has granted us freewill choice, it stands to reason that He chooses not to override it. Why? Because He wants followers who decide for themselves to establish personal relationships and intimate fellowship with Him because they *want* or *choose* to. As with personal and romantic relationships, we want people to love us and want to be around us because they *want* to, not because they *have* to. In the same way, God wants us to love Him freely, not out of predestined obligation.

Partiality?

Some people may think, *What if God allows only certain people to come closer to Him?* After all, He only chose twelve disciples from the masses. He influenced the inner core group for greater nearness and insight with Him. And don't forget, "Jacob I have loved, but Esau I have hated" (Romans 9:13).

Sometimes we indirectly accuse God of playing favorites as our excuse for a lack of intimacy with Him. *Sure, God does incredible things for others and reveals Himself intimately with others, but not with me. I'm the redheaded stepchild sitting in the corner, abandoned and isolated while God interacts with His favorite children. I know He loves me, but He really, r-e-a-l-l-y loves everyone else.* Just because we have this mindset doesn't make it true.

We must look to Scripture for answers about God and partial treatment. Jesus said, "Whoever desires to come after Me, let him deny himself, and take up his cross, and follow Me" (Mark 8:34). He also said, "Whoever comes to Me, and hears My sayings and does them, I will show you whom he is like" (Luke 6:47). Additionally, Jesus promised, "The one who comes to Me I will by no means cast out" (John 6:37). Probably the most famous verse in the Bible says, "For God so loved the world that He gave His only begotten Son, that whoever believes in Him should not perish but have everlasting life" (John 3:16). Then we have the awesome invitation at the end of the Bible: "The Spirit and the bride say, 'Come!' And let him who hears say, 'Come!' And let him who thirsts come. Whoever desires, let him take the water of life freely" (Revelation 22:17).

Did you notice the theme of *whoever* in all those verses? The word *whoever* indicates anyone, not just specifically identified individuals. Also, the action verbs in these verses indicate personal choice of action. To sum it up, free will involves anyone's personal choice to come to Christ or to pursue a closer level of intimacy with Him. Why give freewill choice if that choice is overruled by a partial selection? Both realities cannot coexist.

From this, we confirm the levels of intimacy aren't *preferential* or acts of favoritism. God is not a respecter of people nor does He show partiality (Acts 10:34). Although His ways are far above our understanding and His purpose beyond our comprehension, He is "not willing that any should perish, but that all should come to repentance" (2 Peter 3:9). He offers His love to everyone and extends His presence to all who choose to enter it (Hebrews 4:16). He eagerly awaits the fellowship with all who come to Him in Spirit and truth (John 4:23).

Far from being a sovereign, preferential choice, our individual levels of intimacy with God remain a product of personal choice. We get as close to God as we choose.

Permanence?

There may be a presumption that once achieved, nearness to God is a permanent haven of rest—it requires no further effort on our part. Once we reach spiritual utopia, we are finished with our spiritual journey.

Unfortunately, it isn't permanent until we reach heaven. For now, we live in a fallen, sinful world with many competing distractions and priorities that woo us away from our closeness with God. Even our own seemingly innocent excuses for not putting much effort or focus on it are a clear indication of spiritual erosion. Sin, the carnal flesh, the world, and the Devil are aggressive enemies constantly fighting to keep us from the very thing we desperately need. The battle is ongoing while we are still here on earth.

Finding and maintaining intimacy with God requires constant time, attention, development, and nurturing. Just as in personal or romantic relationships, intimacy depends on individual desire and priority. It bears repeating: each person is as close to God as he or she chooses to be. Each person chooses his or her own level of affection, commitment, priority, and walk of holiness. The sweet intimacy, fellowship, and connection of His presence await us.

Hallelujah, there is coming a day when all who have placed their trust in Jesus Christ will shout, "I shall be satisfied when I awake in Your likeness" (Psalm 17:15). While still here on earth, however, may we passionately pursue the intimacy of His presence each and every day.

Chapter 12

Characteristics of Deepening Intimacy with God

What did the apostle John possess that differentiated him from everyone else, even the other disciples, and promoted such intimacy with Jesus?

In looking at John's life during and after his earthly association with Jesus, as well as his writings years later, we find he developed several critical characteristics. Keep in mind, according to some traditions John and Jesus were cousins. If this is the case, they would have grown up together. John would have had plenty of insider information to downplay or discredit Jesus as Savior of the world and Son of God. And yet John enjoyed the closest relationship with Jesus and encouraged deeper intimacy in his writings.

Some commentators and theologians believe John was much younger than the other disciples. When we first encounter him in Scripture, he is a fisherman, so he was at least old enough to be employed. Jesus started His ministry when He was around thirty years of age. It was customary for a rabbi or teacher to mentor younger men. Presumably, all the disciples could have been in their twenties with John possibly in his late teens. Several times Jesus referred to the disciples as "little children." John must have been younger or in better shape than Peter as he outran Peter to the empty tomb after the resurrection. Finally, since John was old enough to care for the mother of Jesus (John 19:26-27), he was probably at least twenty at the time of the crucifixion. In addition to beginning his relationship with Jesus at an early age, he lived a long time, passing away late in the first century. This means the majority of John's long life was centered on Jesus.

To understand the transformation in John's life, we need to look at him before He knew Jesus. When Jesus called James and John to follow Him, he nicknamed the brothers, "Sons of Thunder" (Mark 3:17). The implication behind this reference is in their zealous, fiery, passionate disposition. We see evidence of this when they asked Jesus to call down fire from heaven to consume an entire village whose residents refused to welcome them (Luke 9:54). But spending time with Jesus transformed John's heated passion. The Son of Thunder became the Apostle of Love. Much of his writing contains descriptions of love and encouragement for Christ followers to demonstrate love in word and deed.

When we look at John's temperament, style, and attitude—coupled with the transformation that took place in his life—we find several traits that reflect and promote intimacy with God. It should encourage us to know we also can develop and nurture these traits on our separate journeys.

Innocent and Deeply Trusting Faith

Jesus often referred to childlike faith. Children usually grasp and believe truth easier than adults who question everything based on their experiences and developed skepticism. As possibly the youngest disciple, John may very well have developed an untarnished friendship and loyalty with Jesus. Think of it as a younger brother looking at his older brother as his hero. And what a hero. Surely, this innocence, openness, and reliant trust contributed to the intimacy they shared.

No matter when we begin a relationship with Jesus, we control the level of trust or faith in Him. Saving faith is much different than sustaining faith. Salvation is a one-time occurrence; sanctification is the journey of a lifetime. Along that journey, trusting Him involves increasingly more impactful choices. Life's decisions offer opportunities to trust God more and more in all areas of life. As with other relationships, intimacy runs parallel with trust. Our level of intimacy with Jesus parallels our level of faith in Him. "Without faith it is impossible to please Him" (Hebrews 11:6). May we develop such childlike faith to trust Him completely and follow Him resolutely—in every area of life, regardless of the circumstances, our developed skepticism, or our preconceived ideas.

Undistracted, Passionate Love

John reveled in the depth of God's love. "Behold what manner of love the Father has bestowed on us, that we should be called children of God!" (1 John 3:1). "Beloved, let us love one another, for love is of God; and everyone who loves is born of God and knows God. He who does not love does not know God, for God is love. If God so loved us, we also ought to love one another" (1 John 4:7-8, 11). Spending time with Jesus transformed the tempestuous Son of Thunder into the Apostle of Love, the Beloved. He wasn't afraid to demonstrate his affection (leaning against Jesus at the Last Supper) or to express his love in his gospel and epistles. As an ardent follower of Jesus, he pursued Him with a passionate love.

The apostle Paul also understood the enormity and marvelousness of God's love. He said it has been poured into our hearts by the Holy Spirit (Romans 5:5). Absolutely nothing can separate us from it (Romans 8:38-39). We cannot imagine the glorious rewards God has planned for those who love Him (1 Corinthians 2:9). The life of faith directly correlates to God's love (Galatians 2:20). God's love exceeds our understanding (Ephesians 3:19). It is the first trait listed as the fruit of the Holy Spirit (Galatians 5:22). Without it, we are truly nothing (1 Corinthians 13).

James, the half-brother of Jesus and a leader of the early church in Jerusalem, added to the accolades of love by saying God will give the crown of life (James 1:2) and an inheritance in the heavenly kingdom (James 2:5) to those who love Him.

As one final point, John confirmed that our obedience to God is evidence of His love being perfected or completed in us (1 John 2:5). If we don't love others, how can we say we love Him? Jesus also said, "If you love me, keep My commandments" (John 14:15). A life filled with passionate love for God will be one that is obedient to God.

A distinction must be made here. Just as there is a world of difference between liking and loving, there is a world of difference between *head* knowledge and *heart* knowledge. The mind sometimes thinks it loves; the heart loves genuinely. The mind may know many facts *about* a perceived loved one. The heart goes deeper to know and be known intimately. We hide God's Word in our hearts not our minds (Psalm 119:11). Why? Because the mind stipulates an "I ought to" mindset; the will mandates an "I have to" mindset. But the heart inspires an "I love to" mindset and lifestyle. By hiding God's Word in my heart, my heart is prompted to obey Him—not because I ought to or have to but because I want to. I desire to. I long to. I want to please my Beloved.

A man and woman involved in a romantic relationship love each other because they want to, not because they should or are coerced. With loving hearts, they seek each other's best interests and passionately unite their hearts. When Jesus resides at the center of our hearts, nothing else distracts us. It is in the heart where holiness takes root. The heart is where commitment and surrender reside. Where logic fails, love prevails.

Why wouldn't we be helplessly and completely in love with Jesus? After all He has done for us, and in view of what He promises us, how can we be anything but recklessly devoted to Him? Apart from Him, we are incapable of love. Unless He loved us first, we couldn't love Him in return (1 John 4:19). By Him, through Him, and for Him, may we love Him gratefully, passionately, and fully. Fostering such depth of love deepens our obedience to Him and intimacy with Him. May we go deeper than others dare going, further than others risk going, and closer than others desire to be. As the apostle Paul exclaimed, "the love of Christ compels us" (2 Corinthians 5:14).

Loyalty When All Others Deserted Jesus

When everyone else forsook Jesus in the Garden of Gethsemane, it is believed John was the young man who followed Him. "Then everyone deserted him and fled. A young man, wearing nothing but a linen garment, was following Jesus. When they seized him, he fled naked, leaving his garment behind" (Mark 14:50-52, NIV). John is also presumed to be the disciple who was known to Caiaphas' family and who brought Peter inside the courtyard when Jesus was first arrested (John 18:15-16). No matter the circumstance or occasion, it doesn't surprise us to find John actively and loyally wanting to be near Jesus.

Jesus rewarded John's loyalty by entrusting His mother, Mary, into his care. From the cross, in excruciating pain and about to die, Jesus saw her and John standing nearby and said to His mother, "Woman, behold your son!" Then to John He said, "Behold your mother!" And from that very moment, John took her to his own home (John 19:25-27). We can envision John tenderly leading Mary away from Calvary to protect her from Jesus' final, agonizing hours.

In addition to trusting John with Jesus' earthly mother, God entrusted him with the Revelation of Jesus Christ—the vision of the end times and glorious insight into His eternal kingdom. Faithful in little, entrusted with much. Loyalty produces intimate reliability and security.

The childhood chorus, "I Have Decided to Follow Jesus," speaks to this point. "Though no one joins me, still I will follow. The world behind me, the cross before me. No turning back, no turning back."[5] Jesus left the glory of heaven to suffer the horror of the cross. And He did it for each person. For me. For you. Why? So we could be reconciled back into relationship and fellowship with Him (2 Corinthians 5:18). Scripture overflows with God's faithfulness. How can we help but be loyal to Him who has been so loving and faithful to us? May we always be fiercely loyal to Him.

Intense Passion for Following and Obeying

John had a zealous temperament. It didn't take much to fire him up. Fortunately, he carried that passion into his obedience to God's Word. Regardless of whether a person's temperament is high-powered or more passive, following and obeying God's Word is something everyone can do. If something is important, it gets prioritized. Temperament just adds a unique flavor.

John recorded Jesus' confirmation that loving Him and obeying Him are synonymous. "Jesus answered and said to him, 'If anyone loves Me, he will keep My word... He who does not love Me does not keep My words'" (John 14:23-24). John continued this theme in his first epistle. "By this we know that we love the children of God when we love God and keep His commandments. For this is the love of God, that we keep His commandments. And His commandments are not burdensome" (1 John 5:2-3). We confirm and deepen our intimacy by living in alignment with God's Word. How can we expect to get closer to God when we ignore, discount, or disobey what He says?

Imagine a personal or romantic relationship where one person constantly resists or rejects what the other person says or wants to do. Sure, love may be expressed deeply and often, but the other person would eventually grow suspicious of such expressions in light of the ongoing struggle. Needless to say, their interaction would hardly be considered a true relationship. And they may as well give up hope of achieving any level of intimacy. As the prophet Amos implied, how can two people walk together unless they are in agreement (Amos 3:3)? Unless two individuals are on the same page, intimacy cannot exist.

Being in God's presence involves aligning ourselves with His Word and yielding to His Holy Spirit. Even maintaining the slightest "iniquity" in our hearts negates our audience with God (Psalm 66:18). There is no negotiation in surrender. We cannot come to God on our own terms. Yielding even ninety-nine percent of ourselves to Him isn't surrender. If He isn't Lord *over* all, He isn't Lord *at* all. Constantly disobeying His Word or resisting His Spirit are signs of spiritual rebellion. When we excuse our behavior and try to negotiate what we will or will not give wholly to Him, we aren't surrendered—and undoubtedly, not even repentant. A repentant person begs for mercy, not his rights or desires. A repentant person seeks forgiveness, not his preference. A repentant person longs for reconciliation with the Father, he doesn't position himself as an equal on the throne of his life. A surrendered person prays, "Not my will but Thine be done." A repentant, surrendered, and transformed person walks in the newness of God's life and intimacy of His presence.

Until we yield everything to Him and obey what He says in His Word, pursuing intimacy with Him will be an ongoing struggle. May we commit to living in obedience to Him as evidence of our love for Him and desire to draw near to Him.

Intense Longing for Fellowship with Jesus

From what we find in the Bible, John wanted to be around Jesus—wherever He was—at all times. He just never knew what unique surprise Jesus would offer next. John realized it was far better to be right next to Jesus than keeping his distance or running off on his own. The more he was in Jesus' presence, the more he loved Him, learned from Him, wanted to be like Him, and desired to please Him.

Being constantly and faithfully at Jesus' side, John experienced things few others did. He saw Jesus transfigured (Matthew 17:1-13). He saw Jesus raise a little girl from the dead (Mark 5:36-43). He participated in a private prayer time on a mountain (Luke 9:28). He sat next to him at the Last Supper—even leaning up against Him (John 13:23-25). He experienced Jesus' agony in the Garden of Gethsemane (Mark 14:32-33). As Jesus was dying on the cross, John was the only disciple there (John 19:26). When Jesus arose from the dead, John was one of the first to arrive at the empty tomb (John 20:3-4).

Undoubtedly, Jesus wouldn't invite to these intimate settings someone who was distracted or resistant. He rewards those who diligently, intentionally, and passionately seek His presence (Hebrews 11:6). May we, "Seek the Lord while He may be found, call upon Him while He is near" (Isaiah 55:6). May we passionately seek and safeguard time alone with Him. May we engage Him in ongoing conversation (1 Thessalonians 5:17) and seek His participation throughout each day. May we start and end each day seeking His guidance and presence in all we say, think, and do. Successful human relationships demand such ongoing communication and interaction. Let's not settle for anything less in our pursuit of intimacy with God.

Intimate Communication with Jesus

On several occasions John came to Jesus, publicly and privately, to ask His opinion. No topic was off limits. There was the time he asked if he and his brother, James, could sit at Jesus' side in His kingdom (Matthew 20:20-22). He angrily asked Jesus if they could call down fire from heaven on a town that refused to allow them to enter it (Luke 9:53-54). Then he privately asked Jesus about the end times (Mark 13:3-4). This makes me wonder if John's curiosity about the end times and Christ's future kingdom was partly why God granted him the Revelation. After all, Jesus did say, "Ask and you shall receive" (John 16:24).

John absorbed every word Jesus said. Actually, Jesus communicated much more than what John included in his gospel and later writings (John 21:25). He accepted Jesus' challenge: "If you abide in Me, and My words abide in you, you will ask what you desire, and it shall be done for you" (John 15:7). John's heart was set on Jesus; Jesus' words found their home in John's heart. We would do well to likewise "hide" God's Word in our hearts (Psalm 119:11). The Holy Spirit can bring it to our recollection when we need it most. This, along with reading God's Word, is how we hear from God. Add prayer to this process, and we have two-way communication. God speaks to us through His Word and Spirit; we speak to Him through prayer and praise.

Honest, unguarded, two-way communication fuels the vulnerability of intimacy. In addition to vulnerability and trust, any human relationship is only as strong as its communication. Without open, honest, and ongoing communication, how can two people know what's going on? How can they comment or engage? In precisely this same manner, open, honest, and ongoing communication with God helps us share what's on our hearts and hear Him respond. Unlike Adam and Eve who made excuses when caught in their sin, may we bring everything—yes, even our sins—before Him immediately, honestly, and passionately. He already knows the thoughts and intents of our hearts (Hebrews 4:12), but He wants our openness and vulnerability. No topic is insignificant, no request too small. In the pursuit of intimacy with God, may we maintain such open, constant conversation with Him.

Genuine Desire to Please His Lord, Master, and Friend

As we read through John's writings, it becomes clear he nurtured and pursued a passionate relationship with Jesus. Though Lord and Master, Jesus was also John's friend. Spending three and a half years with Jesus aligned John's spirit, mind, soul, and body with Jesus' teaching and lifestyle. With his entire being, John wanted to please and honor Jesus. The apostle Paul described this laser-focused attention to pleasing God when he wrote, "No one engaged in warfare entangles himself with the affairs of this life, that he may please him who enlisted him as a soldier" (2 Timothy 2:4).

John was committed to his relationship with Christ from the moment He called him. He was faithfully devoted through Jesus' ministry and crucifixion, even in his race with Peter to see the empty tomb of his risen Friend. Then, to see Christ glorified in heaven in His Revelation—can you imagine John's heart beating faster in anticipation of that glorious reunion? Picture his thrill when he saw the "Lamb as though it had been slain" holding the seven-sealed scroll and then heard all of heaven burst forth in singing, "You are worthy to take the scroll, and to open its seals; for You were slain, and have redeemed us to God by Your blood" (Revelation 5:6, 9). After Jesus said, "Surely I am coming quickly," John exclaimed, "Even so, come, Lord Jesus!" (Revelation 22:20).

In a thriving, romantic relationship, each person has a passionate desire to be in his or her beloved's presence, to please him or her, and anticipate spending time together. How much more intense the fervent believer's desire to be in his Beloved's presence, to please Him, and anticipate spending eternity together in unbroken, unhindered fellowship. That is the essence of intimacy with God. To know and be known by Him intimately for eternity, being forever in His presence. No wonder all heaven worships before Him crying out, "Holy, holy, holy!" (Revelation 4:8). No wonder millions of voices loudly praise Him: "Worthy is the

Lamb who was slain to receive power and riches and wisdom, and strength and honor and glory and blessing!" (Revelation 5:12).

To grasp even the smallest hint of His eternal glory, power, and majesty—then to know He desires a relationship with us and longs for intimacy with us ... how can we resist such love? How can we resist the compelling attraction to run into His sweet embrace, snuggle up next to His heart, drink in His Word, and quiet ourselves in His presence? The apostle Paul summed it up best: "The love of Christ compels us" (2 Corinthians 5:14). His immense love constrains, attracts, and draws us to His side. May we be ever restless until we find our peace in His presence. May the ultimate goal of our lives be to please Him in all we think, say, and do.

Chapter 13

Applying God's Promises

Part of growing in relationship and resting in God's secret place is learning about His promises, then claiming them as our own. By not personalizing them, we remain in the detached aloofness of shallow and casual interaction.

God's Word is full of relational promises that bind His heart to what He says. To personalize what God says is to draw near to His heart. We must move beyond simply *knowing* His promises to *accepting* and *applying* them to our lives, circumstances, and situations. This requires faith and trust in what He says. To question, doubt, or discount what He says, or even place conditions on His promises, is to not believe Him. To believe is to trust implicitly; to disbelieve is to be skeptical and evasive.

For example, we know God says He loves the world and gave His Son so we may be reconciled back to Him. However, some may think, *Yes, universally, He loves everyone but I'm just one insignificant person. I have nothing to offer Him. I've made some serious mistakes in life. Why would He love me? What does that even mean and how does it apply to me?* By discounting what God says, we place faulty human reason above His divine promise. In that perspective, we doubt His love and goodness toward us and question His involvement in our lives. We also greatly devalue ourselves—the very people for whom He sacrificed so much.

Yet God remains faithful to His Word. He says what He means and means what He says. When He says He loves us, that is exactly what He means. He loves us. Unconditionally. Any discomfort that causes is due to our own flawed perceptions, self-judgments, and awareness of the gap between our sinful nature and His holiness. But it in no way discredits, discounts, or disparages God's reality. The best way to approach what God says is to accept it, by faith, at face value.

Imagine one person in a romantic relationship saying, "I love you," and the other person saying, *Surely, you don't mean that. Maybe you like me, but I suspect you certainly don't love me. How can you love me? What's there to love about me?* Obviously, that relationship has credibility, trust, and self-worth issues. The lover expresses true feelings while the doubter overlays misconceptions, self-doubt, and past pain on what is said. But no such issues exist with God. We can trust what He says in His Word—and bring any misconceptions, self-doubt, and pain to Him for healing, restoration, and reconciliation.

In my post-graduate studies, one of my professors had a simple yet profound method of studying the Bible. "What does it say? What does it mean? How does it apply?" To determine how to *apply* scriptural truth to our lives, let's look at a few of God's promises to see what they *say* and what they *mean*.

> *(God) has said, "I will never leave you nor forsake you"* (Hebrews 13:5, parenthesis added).

Most people can understand and acknowledge God's omnipresence. He is everywhere simultaneously. He simply *is*. But quite often, we don't envision Him riding in the car with us, lounging on the sofa next to us, sitting beside us at our jobs, or watching over us while we sleep. It's often easier to consider Him an all-encompassing Being out there somewhere in the universe than to view Him as a "friend who sticks closer than a brother" (Proverbs 18:24).

To admit He is everywhere we are, can be both comforting and frightening. It is comforting to know we are always in His presence, always on His mind, and always in His view. "The eyes of the LORD are in every place, keeping watch on the evil and the good" (Proverbs 15:3). But it can be frightening and heartbreaking to know He is right there beside us when we shoot heroin or drive drunk. Tears flow as He sees His children click through pornographic websites, have sex outside of marriage, curse other drivers in traffic jams, lie without remorse, pull gun triggers in hate, and cheat in business dealings.

If only we would realize God Almighty walks beside us every day, through every circumstance and situation, and hears every conversation. That alone would improve many of our lifestyle choices and reorient our minds to our closeness with Him. The *comfort* of His nearness compels us to draw even closer to Him. The *fear* of His nearness prompts us to repent and forsake (Proverbs 28:13) whatever keeps us from the comfort of His presence.

> *You will keep him in perfect peace, whose mind is stayed on You, because he trusts in You* (Isaiah 26:3).

Frequently, the frenzied busyness of our lives stunts our intimacy with God. We are too busy to spend quality time with Him. Our minds spin out of control regarding all the things we have to do—or aren't getting done. Add to that Satan's whispered deceit and our own discounting voices (*I'm not good enough, worthy enough, whatever enough for God. God doesn't really care about me. God gives others a close sense of Himself, but not me.*) and our minds become fertile ground for spiritual attacks.

For this reason, God instructs us to, "Think on these things" (Philippians 4:8). What things? Things that are true, noble, just, pure, lovely, of good report, virtuous, and praiseworthy. Since the mind is a spiritual battlefield, God encourages us to aggressively train our minds to think and meditate on what aligns with His Word. His truth directly opposes Satan's destructive strategy as well as our self-deprecating, discounting, or doubtful mindsets. That's why He gave us His Word; that's why we should trust and apply it. The heart is deceptive (Jeremiah 17:9); the mind is a battlefield. We need help from Someone bigger than ourselves.

A mind firmly fixed on Jesus is usually not focused on the waves of a surrounding storm. A mind firmly centered on Jesus prioritizes the time to get to know Him more intimately. A mind firmly focused on Jesus rests in His presence, trusting Him to speak truth and orchestrate the associated details of that truth.

Until our minds are set on Him, we remain in the unhealthy state of "a double-minded man" being unstable in all his ways (James 1:8). Yet God promises perfect peace to those who remain focused on Him. Which would we rather have—confused, unstable minds apart from God or minds at perfect peace and rest in His presence? To leverage this promise, we must meet its condition—minds fully fixed on God.

You will make me full of joy in Your presence (Acts 2:28).

We find unspeakable, overflowing joy in God's presence (1 Peter 1:8). Although this verse refers primarily to the future state of being with God in heaven for eternity, it's also an indicator of our present state of intimacy with Him. Spending time with our loving Father, basking in His presence, feasting on His Word, sensing His Spirit within, listening for His loving whisper—all fill our souls with satisfied fulness. Not only does it *fill us* with joy, it is the *source* of our joy. "In Your presence is fulness of joy" (Psalm 16:11).

A large part of joy is rejoicing and praising God. King David, a man after God's own heart (Acts 13:22), knew about the sweet, joyful presence of God. He counselled believers to come into God's presence with thanksgiving (Psalm 95:2) and singing (Psalm 100:2). What a great description for rejoicing. We come to God praising Him for His bountiful blessings. We worship Him for who He is. Our hearts overflow with joy as we thank Him, praise Him, and worship Him. This is also what we'll be doing for eternity so we might want to get really good at it here and now.

Yes, there is fulness of joy in His presence. Are we living joyless lives? If so, let's come into His presence.

Come to Me, all you who labor and are heavy laden, and I will give you rest. Take My yoke upon you and learn from Me, for I am gentle and lowly in heart, and you will find rest for your souls. For My yoke is easy and My burden is light." (Matthew 11:28-30)

God doesn't give us heavy burdens. On the contrary, Jesus said His burden is light. It is Satan who weighs us down with guilt, shame, inferiority complexes, unworthiness, feelings of not being enough, emphasis on trying harder to gain God's acceptance, and reminders of past painful experiences and failures.

In the busyness of life and frantic mindsets, we exhaust ourselves doing what generally is unnecessary. We assault our minds by not politely saying "no" to various involvements, sometimes even in ministry. Just because we may be capable and available to do certain things doesn't mean they are aligned with God's purposes for us. That mindset usually comes from the need to control outcomes or do things the *right* way instead of finding and pursuing what God sovereignly orchestrates and designs.

We become fatigued to the point of burning out and giving up. That's when we are most vulnerable to Satan's attacks. Instead of "bringing every thought into captivity to the obedience of Christ" (2 Corinthians 10:5), we overload our minds with unnecessary doubts, unending lists, unrealistic fears, and unbearable imaginations. As we spin out of control, Jesus stands beside us gently asking to trade our heavy burdens for His rest. His Word tells us to cast all our cares and anxieties on Him because He cares about us (1 Peter 5:7). He asks for our burdens; we can trust Him to handle them. God never intended for us to carry them. Although each problem may not be immediately solved, we can rest assured He walks beside us to carry us through and give the guidance and strength we need, when we need it.

Jesus knows and cares about our spiritual, mental, emotional and physical conditions. Even He, after a wearying time of ministry, invited the disciples to, "Come aside by yourselves to a deserted place and rest a while" (Mark 6:31). Such rest is available to every person (Hebrews 4:1). All it takes is to come into His presence, become authentically vulnerable before Him, and entrust Him with our burdens by leaving them in His capable hands. Then get quiet, and rest.

Be still, and know that I am God; I will be exalted among the nations, I will be exalted in the earth! (Psalm 46:10)

Most of us can't just be still. We have to be busy or have some techno-device in our hands at all times. Checking this online status. Researching that tidbit of information. Who said what, when, and where? We are on information overload. If God wanted to whisper something to us, we would either be too busy to notice or too distracted to hear.

Thankfully, in His love, He doesn't leave us where we are. He continually calls us to be still and know He is God. He is still on the throne. He is still in control. He is still available for relationship and intimacy.

The meaning behind "be still" is to stop, cease, be faint or feeble, be idle, leave, let alone, or let go. In essence, it means to stop being so busy being busy. It's a call to let go of our burdens, concerns, and distractions, get alone, and be motionless and quiet. For many people, this leads to boredom or falling sleep. Even the slightest break from constant busyness allows our exhausted bodies and minds to rest. Yet it highlights the need to discipline ourselves regarding the need for internal and external quietness.

A major part of abiding in God's secret place of intimacy is the quieting of our minds and being still in His presence. The story of Jesus visiting Mary and Martha (Luke 10:38-42) describes Martha as being "distracted" by many things. She busily rushed about to ensure everything in the house was in order. But Mary sat at Jesus' feet and just listened to Him, absorbing His presence and message. Jesus later confirmed Mary had chosen the better option. Instead of hurriedly rushing about making sure every detail was covered, she chose to come into His presence, quiet herself before Him, and hear His voice.

Dissecting Psalm 46:10

As an excellent example of being still in God's secret place, we can elaborate on Psalm 46:10 by incorporating it into the story of Mary and Martha.

- *Be* – As opposed to *do*. Be authentically in His presence (Mary) instead of busily distracted by activities and thoughts (Martha). Imagine yourself sitting peacefully beside Him in a boat on the calm Sea of Galilee or at His feet in a grassy meadow. Just the two of you are there, and He is speaking specifically to you.

- **Still** – Calm your frenzied, cluttered mind and busy hands. Relinquish control of your thoughts to Him. Allow Him to breathe "peace be still" across the doubts and fears of past disappointments, pain, and failures. Release your current deadlines and to-do lists. Get motionless and quiet in His presence.

- **And** – In addition to being present and calming your mind, prepare yourself for something else. Avoid the temptation to rush ahead of Him or think you know what He is saying to you. Be expectant in His presence, listening intently to His every word.

- **Know** – Just as Mary was present and still, she was teachable as she listened to Jesus. Open your mind to discover, accept, and understand new things He shares with you. Avoid simply knowing many things *about* Him at the expense of knowing Him intimately.

- **That I am God** – Discover His identity, character, presence, heart, purpose, and intention. To know Him fully is to trust Him, rely on Him, and become vulnerable before Him. These all promote deeper intimacy. Let God be God; you be you.

If we cannot be quiet by ourselves, how do we expect to be quiet before God? If we don't control and shut off the noise in our heads, how can we expect to hear from God? I've found that God usually doesn't shout over competing voices—He quietly waits His turn for our attention. May our restlessness encourage us to drown out every other voice and find our rest in His presence every day.

As we quietly read through God's promises, may we ask the Holy Spirit to show us how to apply them to whatever specific area of life needs them most. When He does, may we accept it and obey. With the piercing, penetrating Word of God (Hebrews 4:12) and the guiding truth of the Spirit of God (John 16:13), we have the insight and power necessary to transform our lives while moving closer, becoming nearer, to God.

Chapter 14

Realigning Personal Mindsets to God's Truth

One of the most important yet difficult steps on the journey of deeper intimacy with God is a change of personal mindset (2 Corinthians 10:3-5). After all, how can we get to know who He truly is, how He thinks, and how He acts if we clutter our minds with pre-conceived ideas? By associating this to human relationships, we see how individual mindsets move from a single-focused, selfish view to each person thinking of the other person. For any relationship to thrive, all reservations, arguments, hesitancies, imaginations, false perceptions, safe places against previous trauma—everything—must be tossed aside to make room for new truth. How can we learn new things about someone if our minds are already made up?

God encourages us to remove or destroy all "arguments and every high thing that exalts itself against the knowledge of God, bringing every thought into captivity to the obedience of Christ" (2 Corinthians 10:5). We must forcibly and repeatedly release, resist, and destroy anything that conflicts with who God is, what He says about Himself and us, and how He interacts with us. That includes our preferential, traditional, and comfortable mindsets.

Over the years, it's surprising how much misinformation we pick up about God from friends, teachers, youth pastors, church leaders, parents, college professors, bosses, television shows, self-help books—all tainted with each particular perspective. To see the impact of all this, imagine a man is interested in a certain woman. If he asked everyone within his social circle about her and researched every online venue, how many differing opinions would he find? He would receive much information *about* her, but wouldn't really get to *know* her. Instead of getting lost in all these biased perspectives, why not just spend time *with* her getting to know her for himself? Similarly, intimacy with God only flourishes when we align our thoughts, perceptions, imaginations, perspectives, and beliefs with what God reveals in His eternal, unchanging, unbiased, trustworthy Word. Instead of taking someone else's opinion, why not spend time alone with God ourselves?

One example of a mindset needing to be renewed is the tendency to become our own worst critics. We discount our value and base our self-esteem on how we feel or on the world's standards. But instead of allowing such a self-defeating mindset, we must reject such thoughts and proclaim God's truth that we are "fearfully and wonderfully made" (Psalm 139:13-16), handmade by God Himself in His image (Genesis 1:26). By doing so, we get an immediate lift in our spirits and sense of self-worth. No matter our shortcomings, faults, and feelings, we are wise to recognize, accept, and claim who God says we are.

Inaccurate mindsets may be due to a lack of knowledge. If we don't know we can have deeper fellowship and intimacy with God, how will we know to pursue it? Stubborn mindsets may be the result of past painful relationship experiences that we overlay onto our relationship with God. If people we trusted betrayed or abused that trust, we may be less willing to be as vulnerable as necessary for true relational intimacy—even with God. Emotional trauma may also be a hindering mindset. If authority figures abused or abandoned us, we will be skeptical of God's authority over us.

These are just a few examples of how our mindsets can prevent deeper spiritual intimacy with God. They represent a small sample of situations where thoughts need to be "taken captive" and replaced with God's truth. As difficult as it may be, as entrenched as the mindsets may be, as fearful as we are about releasing them, the journey of deepening intimacy with God requires their realignment. Instead of believing our own false narrative, may we embrace God and His absolute truth. May we sit quietly in His presence, with His Word, allowing Him to surround and fill us with Himself.

If there are still inner struggles even after we've deliberately surrendered all to God, a hidden issue may lurk in the shadows of our subconscious minds. Deception is such a misleading thing. It keeps us believing something is true when in fact it isn't. May we cry out to God as David did, "Who can understand his errors? Cleanse me from secret faults" (Psalm 19:12). We often don't see what's in our blind spots—something probably near and dear to us—that keeps us from God's fullness. To help offset such deception, may we honestly and repeatedly pray, "Search me, O God, and know my heart; try me, and know my anxieties; and see if there is any wicked way in me, and lead me in the way everlasting" (Psalm 139:23-24). Then, whatever God reveals, repent and release it to Him. Even if He doesn't reveal specifics, release the hidden and unknown to Him. Proactively yield to Him those subconscious blind spots. Give Him permission to remove whatever is necessary to continue His transforming work.

Let's look at a few more misconceptions, false narratives, and blind-spot mindsets that hinder deeper intimacy with God.

God is Not an Absent or Abusive Parent

I am enough. God may have spoken everything else into creation, but He handmade humans. This is a much more intimate association. He gave each person unique fingerprints, personality traits, talents, gifts, and skills that align with the specific purposes He intended for them. He also gave His Son Jesus to die for us to reconcile us to Himself. He designed the way possible for us to have a relationship with Him and enjoy personal, intimate fellowship with Him. Additionally, He is love. As such, He loves each person incredibly, beyond our understanding. This makes us incredibly valuable. Yes, we are enough.

We don't have to chase God around for attention or acceptance. God is the Great I AM. He is who He is. He is the same yesterday, today, and forever (Hebrews 13:8). He never changes (Malachi 3:6). God is omnipresent, simultaneously everywhere—no one is abandoned or isolated. He is right there beside each of us. There are no subtle variations, sudden changes, or surprises with God's character (James 1:17). He loves us unconditionally and wants intimate relationships with each of us (John 3:16). We don't have to wonder where He is or chase Him down for attention or acceptance. He is right here with us, patiently waiting at each heart's door (Revelation 3:20). Upon opening our hearts, we begin the journey into His secret, peaceful, shaded, secure place of intimacy.

God is reliable, trustworthy, and protective for all, not just a select few. God has no favorites (Ephesians 6:9). All throughout the Old Testament, He condemned the practice of partiality. So why would we presume He would do that with us? Since God is constant in character, He doesn't show partiality (Deuteronomy 10:17; Romans 2:11). "God shows personal favoritism to no man" (Galatians 2:6). Actually, according to James 2:9, showing partiality is a sin. In His omniscience He already foreknows who will accept and reject Him, but He is "not willing that any should perish but that all should come to repentance" (2 Peter 3:9). There is no secret, divine agenda that excludes anyone from His love and salvation or from intimacy in His presence. By understanding His constancy, we can trust Him, rely fully on Him, and become wholly open and vulnerable with Him.

God is Not a Cosmic Cop

We don't have to be good enough. God doesn't want us to clean ourselves up or get our act together before He will agree to spend time with us. He isn't a cosmic cop waiting for us to slip up so He can smack us. Furthermore, He already knows we cannot clean ourselves up. That's why He sovereignly orchestrated salvation, forgiveness, and cleansing from before time began (2 Timothy 1:9). He also removed the need for self-incriminating thoughts or feelings by saying, "There is none righteous, no, not one" (Romans 3:10). He already knows our sinful state, yet loves us still. Any self-defeating or unworthy thoughts we may have don't come from God. Our adversary, the Devil, the father of all lies and deception (John 8:44), accuses us before God (Revelation 12:10) and tries to instill a spirit of fear in us (2 Timothy 1:7a). But God gives us love, power, and soundness of mind (2 Timothy 1:7b). He invests such amazing gifts because He loves us and knows we need Him against the attacks from our adversary and our own mindsets. Only through His goodness and strength, not our own, can we stand before Him in reverent confidence.

God wants us to succeed, not fail. This may surprise some people. All too often we perceive God from a negative perspective. *Thou shalt not ... can't do this ... can't do that ... live in fear of Him judging us for ... too hard to live up to His standards ...* Here is a mind-blowing secret. God already knows we cannot live up to His standards or please Him on our own. In His holiness, He already stands across the "great gulf" that our sin created (Luke 16:26) beckoning us to come to Him.

When Luke, a physician, wrote the gospel that bears his name, he used a medical term in describing the "great gulf" in the story of the rich man and the beggar named Lazarus. Both men died. Lazarus went to heaven (also called Abraham's bosom), the rich man went to flaming torment. As the rich man agonized in his eternal flames, he cried out to Abraham asking him to send Lazarus with even a little cooling water to provide some temporary relief. Abraham said, "Between us and you there is a great gulf fixed, so that those who want to pass from here to you cannot, nor can those from there pass to us." The medical definition behind the word used to describe *gulf* is "an open wound."[6] Wow! What a spot-on description of our sin. An open, unhealed, festering, stinking wound. And yet it was for that specific wound Christ came to earth and sacrificed His life. He brings healing and abundant life for those who trust and accept Him through faith.

In offering such an enormous investment, how can we ever think God wants us to fail instead of succeed? He helps us succeed not only in this life but in the next life as well. He disciplines when we disobey and stray from His path, but He does even that in love (Hebrews 12:6) and for our benefit (Psalm 119:71). If He left us in our sin, we could have no relationship, much less close fellowship with Him. But He loves us too much to leave us where He found us. That alone should convince us of His desire for ongoing and deepening intimacy with us.

Barriers to Intimacy Are Not God's Fault

Any real or perceived barriers to intimacy with God aren't His fault. He has done everything necessary to enable a personal relationship and intimate interaction with Him. No matter our feelings, lack of trust, or negative thoughts, God desires open, honest, and ongoing intimacy with us. We just need to get out of our heads, stop hiding behind excuses, deception, and past experiences. and take Him at His Word.

To help explain the frustrating aspect of doubting God, consider a couple involved in a romantic relationship. The man loves the woman deeply and longs for the emotional connection, vulnerability, and exclusivity of intimacy. Not physical intimacy, but deeper relational intimacy. The woman, however, is clueless about a closer, more meaningful, more relatable level of relational intimacy. She is fine with the relationship as it is—comfortable, convenient, even committed. Imagine if the woman told us the following:

> I'm in a fantastic relationship with the most wonderful person. Someone who loves me passionately, fully, and unconditionally. Someone who is always there for me—to pick me up when I fall, to listen to me gripe. Someone who does everything possible to meet my every need. I truly enjoy being loved so much. Being the center of his attention, receiving his affection, enjoying his supportive affirmation.

> Because he loves me so much, I can (and do) act unlovely at times, yet his love is not withdrawn nor has it grown cold. I can (and do) selfishly withhold myself at times, yet he is always in-the-moment for me. I can (and do) take him for granted, yet he assures and affirms me every day.

> Even though he is always there for me, sometimes I don't really talk with him. You see, my other priorities consume my mind and time. Sometimes I take from him without so much as a,

"thank you," but he understands my heart. Sometimes I get close to him, but usually it's because everyone else has either turned their back on me, disappointed me, can't help me, or don't have time for me. But from my perspective, it's a great relationship. I take and give little in return even though he freely gives me everything. He is my constant, encouraging companion. Quite often, I've flat-out ignored him; still, his love, his time, and his attention are always mine.

In all honesty, I seldom consider how my actions hurt him. Periodically, I may begrudgingly mumble, "I'm sorry," when I've done something really bad. But for the most part, I take full advantage of the freedom he gives to pursue my own interests— without really asking what he wants to do. I find myself always complaining to him, even though he always speaks tenderly to me.

I know he will always support me even though I don't spend much time with him. When he wants something from me, I don't always give it; but, of course, I expect his full attention to my desires. When I don't spend time with him or give him anything in return, he doesn't say ugly things about it or hold it against me. He simply whispers his reassurance. When we fight or have our disagreements, it is usually just me pitching a fit about not getting my way or about the unfairness of my life. But he is amazingly patient, supportive, loving, and kind.

Sometimes I fall asleep in his arms. Most often I fall asleep without so much as a "good night." But when I wake up in the morning, I know he'll be right there beside me. I hope he doesn't stop loving me because I don't know what I'd do or how I'd live without him. Isn't he the greatest? Who wouldn't want a relationship as great as this?

I suspect few people would want, much less stay in, such a one-sided relationship. As a matter of fact, some of us would enjoy having a candid conversation with her about how selfish, cold, indifferent, and clueless she is.

Now, go back and read her comments again. But this time, consider it from the perspective that the man in the story is God and the other person is me or you. How does that change the narrative? Hopefully, it gives a clearer view of how incredibly God longs for more of us—a deeper connection, a closer communion, a more open heart-to-heart fellowship. He has done all He can. The quality of the relationship is up to us.

If this pricks your conscience as it has mine, please don't let it depress or discourage you. Instead, do something about it. As with any quality personal or romantic relationship worth having, it takes openness, confession of wrong, willingness for a deeper vulnerability, and the time invested in being together, learning more about each other, sharing matters of the heart. The conversation we can have with God may sound like this:

> *God, please show me any hesitancy to trust You, any uncertainty to rely on You, and any resistance to be vulnerable with You. You know me better than I know myself—my fears, inadequacies, emotional wounds, insecurities, hang-ups, everything. Please help me release them all to You. Strengthen me to rely on You personally, not merely trust You generally. Embrace me with Your grace, reassure me with Your love, and comfort me with Your peace. I open myself to You and take You at Your Word. I am committed to a closer walk and deeper intimacy with You. Thank You for your eternal, loving, safe, and secure presence. Help me to consistently meet You there. Amen.*

After praying this, then personalize God's promises. A great place to start is acknowledging, "Truly our fellowship is with the Father and with His Son Jesus Christ" (1 John 1:3). Heaven is our throne room; our audience is divine. How awesome is that? Now that is a great relationship and fellowship!

As we read God's Word, may we accept and claim what He says. If He says He loves the world, believe that includes you. When He says He will never abandon us, believe that He is right there beside you at all times. Trusting God includes personally relying on everything He says.

Chapter 15

Moving from Begging to Praising

In Acts 3:1-10, we find the story of a man who was lame from birth. His family (or friends) carried him to the Beautiful Gate just outside the temple area in Jerusalem. From there, he could beg for money from those going into the temple to pray or participate in other religious rituals. He may have expected to prey on the softened hearts of the people prepared to spend time with God. But his expectations would be far exceeded one divinely appointed day.

As Peter and John went to the temple to pray, they heard this lame man begging. They probably knew him, had seen him there frequently, and knew what he wanted. But God longed to give this man something for which he hadn't yet asked or even imagined receiving.

In the same way, the Holy Spirit interacts with us when we pray (Romans 8:26-27). Quite often, we ask for what we can only conceptualize based on our current reality. We pray for immediate relief or answers. But behind the scenes, the Holy Spirit "helps in our weaknesses" because "we do not know what we should pray for as we ought." How comforting to know the Holy Spirit intercedes for us before God the Father. And God the Father, "who searches the hearts," knows the mind of the Spirit because He intercedes for us "according to the will of God."

Notice, the Spirit prays for us according to God's will, not ours. Just like this lame man, we may be asking rather passionately for something dear to our heart, but the Holy Spirit represents us before heaven's throne with something far greater. If we could tune our ears to the heavenly realm, the divine conversation may sound something like this:

Nate praying: *God, I really wish You would give me a quick answer to prayer regarding my unemployment. I need a job fast to have the money to feed my family. You promised to supply my every need, and this is my present need. So, I'm asking You to provide this to me quickly. Amen.*

Holy Spirit interceding before God the Father: *Yes, Nate is asking for a job. But we both know his greater need—patience and reliance on Your will. Please allow this circumstance to strengthen his faith and build his utmost trust in You. Allow Me to continue working on his inward growth before meeting his outward need. Your ultimate will is to prepare Nate for eternity not merely provide for him on earth. Once he has prioritized the world to come, he will be better prepared to meet the challenges of this present world. Let's continue lovingly transforming him in these circumstances—for this I graciously intercede. Amen.*

Notice the difference between what we see, feel, experience, and pray for and what the Holy Spirit prays on our behalf. Notice the difference between what we think we need in the immediate, temporal world and the external significance of God's overall will for us.

If we are completely honest, we've prayed sincerely about things for which we thanked God afterward for unanswered prayers. *God, I really want this job.* Then we find out the boss is a tyrant. *God, I really want this house.* Then we find out it's a money pit. *God, I really see me and this person together for life.* But as time passes, we realize a relationship would have been disastrous. God often protects us with unanswered prayers because our prayers don't align with His perfect will for us.

Knowing God sees our situations far differently than we do shouldn't minimize the urgency of our prayers and needs. Nor does it imply we should never bring requests before God. It just opens our hearts and minds to the realization that God may have something far greater in mind. Something that exceeds what we can think or ask. The lame beggar outside the temple learned that lesson from Peter and John.

After explaining they had no money to give him, the discouraged man shouted his pleas to other people. But Peter had none of that. He said, "In the name of Jesus Christ of Nazareth, rise up and walk" (Acts 3:6). Immediately, the man felt his legs and feet surge with foreign strength. Leaping to his feet, he jumped around and praised God.

The lame man went from begging for what he thought he *wanted* to praising God for what he *needed*, but hadn't asked for. He knew the immediate need of money. But he never imagined walking. Yet that is the very thing God granted him that day.

In my prayer time with God, I used to spend the majority of time going over a long list of requests for myself, my family, my friends, my church, my country, the ministries in which I was involved—the *usual* and *expected*. It never crossed my mind to, "be still and know He is God," to simply sit in His presence and await the *unexpected* and *supernatural*. Just like the lame beggar, I usually have no idea what God wants to do in and through me.

Over the years and through various negative experiences resulting from what I believed I *needed* from God, I have learned the benefit of praying, "Thy will be done," instead of, "Father give me … grant me … if You would only do …" Instead of asking for the *usual* and *expected*, I now find myself anticipating the *unexpected* and *supernatural*. I know God, as my loving, heavenly Father, knows what is best for me—even though my heart, mind, and desires may want something else.

Continuing our story, we later find this same beggar holding on to Peter and John in misguided gratitude. His overjoyed response brought people's attention to Peter and John instead of to God, the source of his healing. He overlooked Peter's statement, "In the name of Jesus Christ," and focused on Peter as the source of blessing.

In similar fashion, I find myself thanking other people for the blessings God grants me. That job promotion, pay increase, personal endorsement, new car, better job, new ministry opportunity—whatever it is. I often express my gratitude to the individuals involved yet frequently overlook that promotion comes from the Lord (Psalm 75:6-7) and every good gift comes from God (James 1:17).

For the most part, God sovereignly orchestrates His will through people. And we should always thank those who bless us. But the primary focus of our praise for answered prayer should always be toward God. An intimate relationship with Him demands a primary and consistent focus on the Lover of our souls. If a wife gushed over the florist who prepared the rose bouquet her husband gave her, it would be a thoughtful, though misguided, response. The florist simply prepared and enabled the husband's loving desire toward his wife. The essence of intimacy involves the response directed toward the beloved. Our praise should always be pointed toward God.

Intimacy Through Praise and Worship

Scripture overflows with encouragement to praise God. Instead of filling our quiet times with begging for this natural request or that expected desire, may we spend it praising God for His love, presence, mercy, favor, faithfulness, provision, salvation, new life, greatness, victory over sin, victory over death, patience, wisdom, comfort, grace, transformation, majesty, Word, deliverance, protection, forgiveness, blessings, sovereign orchestration, unanswered prayers, and whatever else the Holy Spirit brings to mind. Read over this list slowly and imagine life without God's faithful blessings. Then thank Him in grateful praise.

Here are a few reminders to praise God at all times in spite of our circumstances. In reading them aloud during daily devotional times, may they lead our hearts to worship—and increase our sense of God's sweet and awesome presence.

- I will praise the LORD according to His righteousness, and will sing praise to the name of the LORD Most High. (Psalm 7:17)

- I will call upon the LORD, who is worthy to be praised. (Psalm 18:3)

- Those who seek Him will praise the LORD. (Psalm 22:26)

- The LORD is my strength and my shield; my heart trusted in

Him, and I am helped; therefore my heart greatly rejoices, and with my song I will praise Him. (Psalm 28:7)

- Sing praise to the LORD, you saints of His, and give thanks at the remembrance of His holy name. (Psalm 30:4)

- O LORD my God, I will give thanks to You forever. (Psalm 30:12)

- Rejoice in the LORD, O you righteous! For praise from the upright is beautiful. (Psalm 33:1)

- I will bless the LORD at all times; His praise shall continually be in my mouth. (Psalm 34:1)

- He has put a new song in my mouth—praise to our God. (Psalm 40:3)

- Sing praises to God, sing praises! Sing praises to our King, sing praises! For God is the King of all the earth; sing praises with understanding. (Psalm 47:6-7)

- To You, O my Strength, I will sing praises; for God is my defense, my God of mercy. (Psalm 59:17)

- All the earth shall worship You and sing praises to You; they shall sing praises to Your name. (Psalm 66:4)

- It is good to give thanks to the LORD, and to sing praises to Your name, O Most High; to declare Your loving kindness in the morning, and Your faithfulness every night. (Psalm 92:1-2)

- For the LORD is great and greatly to be praised. (Psalm 96:4)

- Shout joyfully to the LORD, all the earth; break forth in song, rejoice, and sing praises. (Psalm 98:4)

- Enter into His gates with thanksgiving, and into His courts with praise. Be thankful to Him, and bless His name. (Psalm 100:4)

- I will sing of mercy and justice; to You, O LORD, I will sing praises." (Psalm 101:1)

- "Bless the LORD, O my soul! O LORD my God, You are very great: You are clothed with honor and majesty. (Psalm 104:1)

- Praise the LORD! Oh, give thanks to the LORD, for He is good! For His mercy endures forever. (Psalm 106:1)

- I will greatly praise the LORD with my mouth. (Psalm 109:30)

- Praise the LORD! Praise, O servants of the LORD, praise the name of the LORD! From the rising of the sun to its going down, the LORD's name is to be praised. (Psalm 113:1, 3)

- His merciful kindness is great toward us, and the truth of the LORD endures forever. Praise the LORD! (Psalm 117:2)

- Oh, give thanks to the LORD, for He is good! For His mercy endures forever. (Psalm 118:1)

- Praise the LORD, for the LORD is good; sing praises to His name, for it is pleasant. (Psalm 135:3)

- I will praise You with my whole heart. (Psalm 138:1)

- Great is the LORD and greatly to be praised; and His greatness is unsearchable. (Psalm 145:3)

- While I live I will praise the LORD; I will sing praises to my God while I have my being. (Psalm 146:2)

- Praise the LORD! For it is good to sing praises to our God; for it is pleasant, and praise is beautiful. (Psalm 147:1)

- Let the high praises of God be in their mouth. (Psalm 149:6)

- Let everything that has breath praise the Lord. Praise the Lord! (Psalm 150:6)

- Praise the LORD, call upon His name; declare His deeds among the peoples, make mention that His name is exalted. Sing to the LORD, for He has done excellent things. (Isaiah 12:4-5)

- Sing to the LORD! Praise the LORD! (Jeremiah 20:13)

- You shall eat in plenty and be satisfied, and praise the name of the LORD your God, who has dealt wondrously with you. (Joel 2:26)

- Be anxious for nothing, but in everything by prayer and supplication, with thanksgiving, let your requests be made known to God. (Philippians 4:6)

- Continue earnestly in prayer, being vigilant in it with thanksgiving. (Colossians 4:2)

- Proclaim the praises of Him who called you out of darkness into His marvelous light. (1 Peter 2:9b)

- Amen! Blessing and glory and wisdom, thanksgiving and honor and power and might, be to our God forever and ever. Amen. (Revelation 7:12)

Heartfelt adoration, praise, and appreciation from one person in a relationship toward the other goes a long way to deepen their relational intimacy. In a similar way, when we fill our mouths, hearts, and minds with praise and gratitude toward God instead of bombarding Him with constant requests, our thoughts shift from self-centeredness to God-centeredness. Our attention shifts from our requests to Him—from what we want Him to do (performance) to who He is (Person). When we understand, admit, and proclaim His greatness, we may find our requests becoming less urgent or significant. And the intimacy we experience grows to a deeper level of appreciation and satisfaction.

If we want to get closer to God and enjoy a nearer sense of His presence, then let us praise Him!

Chapter 16

Making the Commitment

In dating relationships, the time and occasion eventually arrive to "define the relationship." Yes, the often-dreaded DTR. This is when one person wants to make the relationship exclusive. *Are we just having fun or do you see us going the distance? Is this just a friendship or is it more? Are we happy just enjoying each other's company, doing things together, or are we building toward something more permanent and exclusive?*

Obviously, if the response is less than expected, the *friendationship* may quickly come to an end. For the one looking for a more serious level, anything superficial is no longer acceptable. *Why waste time pursuing a relationship that isn't going anywhere?* For the one who is content with the current level of convenient companionship, a deeper level may be the furthest thing from his or her mind. *Why can't we just be friends and keep enjoying what we have? We're having fun, right? I just don't see us getting romantically involved. Can we just continue dating with no deeper expectations?*

Thankfully, God desires deep and exclusive intimacy with us. He is not looking for superficial companionship. Jesus explained the commitment necessary for a devoted, exclusive relationship with Him. "If anyone desires to come after Me, let him deny himself, and take up his cross daily, and follow Me" (Luke 9:23).

Self-denial, sacrifice, and surrender.

Relationally speaking, that involves shifting from individualism to mutualism. From self-indulgence to seeking the other's best interest. From doing what one person wants to yielding to the best for the relationship. Regarding intimacy with God, it means yielding whatever is holding us back from a deeper walk with Him. Giving ourselves wholeheartedly to Him. Aggressively pursuing Him through obedience, reading His Word, and spending quality time alone with Him.

In defining the relationship with God, we already know His heart. He wants an exclusive relationship. He wants it to go the distance. He desires more than a superficial interaction. He loves unconditionally and sacrificed Himself to enable such a relationship and fellowship. It is entirely up to us to determine our level of DTR. Are we ready and willing? Will we commit ourselves to spend quality time with Him? Will we prioritize a deeper walk with Him? Is there anyone or anything distracting us from exclusiveness with Him—and are we willing to give it up?

May we realize the awesome privilege He offers. Just imagine, the sovereign Creator of everything in this infinite universe longs for intimacy with us. He who flung the galaxies into space, formed the thinnest membrane of our cellular structure, and holds it all in His nail-scarred hands, wants to spend time with us. How can we resist such compelling love? What else are we waiting for before yielding and running into His embrace? What prevents us from starting and nurturing intimate time in His presence?

He awaits us.

More specifically, He awaits you.

Don't worry about others, what they may think, or their spiritual experiences. God may be calling you to a closer walk of holiness. You may have sensed a deeper longing for intimacy than others even imagined. You may be willing to invest more than others even have. As wedding vows proclaim, forsake all others and commit yourself to the Lover of your soul. The invitation is open to all. Yet you are the one willing and ready to walk that committed journey while others may be content with superficial levels of companionship.

I encourage you to run to God's secret place. Commit yourself to the pursuit of intimacy with Him. Not out of obligation or fear. Not so you can rattle off a mile-long list of prayer requests. But so you can rest in His presence, quiet yourself before Him, hear His whisper, and sense His heart.

Just as it happens in loving human relationships, once you experience a mere moment of His presence, you'll long for more.

I pray you will find and maintain incredible intimacy with God in His secret place.

Endnotes

1) John Phillips, *Exploring Proverbs – Volume One*, (Kregel Publications, 2002), 554.

2) *Rock of Ages*, Public Domain, https://hymnary.org/text/rock_of_ages_cleft_for_me_let_me_hide, accessed July 26, 2021.

3) *Sitting at the Feet of Jesus*, Public Domain, https://library.timelesstruths.org/music/Sitting_at_the_Feet_of_Jesus, accessed May 23, 2021.

4) Is the ACTS Formula for Prayer a Good Way to Pray? https://www.gotquestions.org/ACTS-prayer.html, accessed June 1, 2021.

5) *I have Decided to Follow Jesus,* Public Domain, https://library.timelesstruths.org/music/I_Have_Decided_to_Follow_Jesus, accessed February 3, 2021.

6) John Phillips, *Exploring the Gospel of Luke – An Expository Commentary*, (Kregel Publications, 2005), 221.

About the Author

A lifelong student of Scripture, Nate Stevens has also enjoyed a banking career in a variety of leadership roles. He is the author of:

Matched 4 Life (book and workbook)
Deck Time with Jesus
Transformed: Until Christ is Formed in You
Conformed: Into the Likeness of Christ
Informed: Living by God's Absolute Truth

He is also a contributing author on several of the Moments Books series (*Billy Graham Moments, Romantic Moments, Divine Moments, Spoken Moments, Christmas Moments, Stupid Moments, and Broken Moments*).

He writes online articles for ChristianDevotions.us and KingdomWinds.com as well as several other ministries. Additionally, he co-founded and leads Fusion, a Christian singles ministry. A popular speaker and teacher at conferences, seminars and Bible study groups, he speaks on a wide variety of topics.

Nate has two adult children. He and his wife, Karen, live near Charlotte, North Carolina.

Follow Nate and find more resources at: www.natestevens.net

Made in the USA
Columbia, SC
28 October 2022

70178093R00070